AF168016

Images of Loughborough and District

A commemorative bell hanging in the Carillon Tower at Queen's Park, Loughborough.

The Carillon Tower in Queen's Park, Loughborough. It was designed and built on the instructions of Sir Walter Tapper in the years 1922–23, to record all those people who lost their lives during World War One. The height of the tower is 151ft. From the balcony at the top of the building the whole of Loughborough can be seen, and the views out into Charnwood Forest are excellent. It houses 47 bells made by Taylors of Loughborough and was the first grand carillon built in Great Britain. It is open to the public and contains a very fine museum selection on three floors.

Images of
Loughborough
and District

TREVOR HICKMAN

breedon **books**
PUBLISHING

First published in Great Britain in 2009 by The Breedon Books Publishing Company Limited, Breedon House,
3 The Parker Centre, Derby, DE21 4SZ

This paperback edition published in Great Britain in 2014 by DB Publishing, an imprint of JMD Media Ltd

© TREVOR HICKMAN, 2009

All rights reserved. No part of this publication may be reproduced, stored in a retrieval system, or transmitted in
any form, or by any means, electronic, mechanical, photocopying, recording or otherwise without the prior
permission in writing of the copyright holders, nor be otherwise circulated in any form or binding or cover other
than which it is published and without a similar condition being imposed on the subsequent publisher.

A catalogue record for this book is available from the British Library.
Thomas Bewick's wood engraving Hunting with Fox Hounds.

Title page: *Thomas Bewick's wood engraving* On the way to market.

By the same author
Historic Cheeses: Leicestershire, Stilton & Stichelton

ISBN 978-1-78091-406-0

Printed and bound in the UK by Copytech (UK) Ltd Peterborough

Contents

Quorn, 1879.

Introduction

In 1999 Breedon Books published *Images of Loughborough*, containing a selection of photographs held in the Loughborough Library's local studies collection. The success of that volume has led to the compilation of this new book covering the districts around Loughborough. The photographs and illustrations have been selected from my own collection of historic images. The book should not be considered a definitive history of the area, but I hope the choice of interesting historical images of Leicestershire will prove of value to local historians with an interest in the area. Occasionally I have used modern photographs to enhance the selection, and in some places I have juxtaposed 21st-century photographs with 19th-century images of the same location.

While working on the book I made a number of journeys around the district with the help of my granddaughter, Amy Grech. Within these pages can be found references to the history of methods of travel through this most interesting area of middle England. The publication is divided into five chapters, with emphasis on the highway. In 1675 John Ogilby produced the first atlas showing all the main roads throughout England. It was a large, cumbersome book, ideal in a library, but it was not much use while travelling on the back of a horse. Many books were torn to pieces and the relevant pages were folded up and used as travellers' maps. It was not until 1720 that Emanuel Bowen published the first usable road atlas. The engravings were produced in such a way that the user, riding on horseback, could see all the relevant reference points on either side of the highway.

For many thousands of years the main methods of travel over long distances had been on foot or on horseback. Wheeled transport existed, but it could only be used on well-maintained roadways. During the Roman occupation fine roadways were laid out, but when the Romans departed, their highways fell into

An engraving of a packhorse with the wicker panniers carrying goods for sale. The eyes of the horse have been covered to prevent it walking away while bartering takes place.

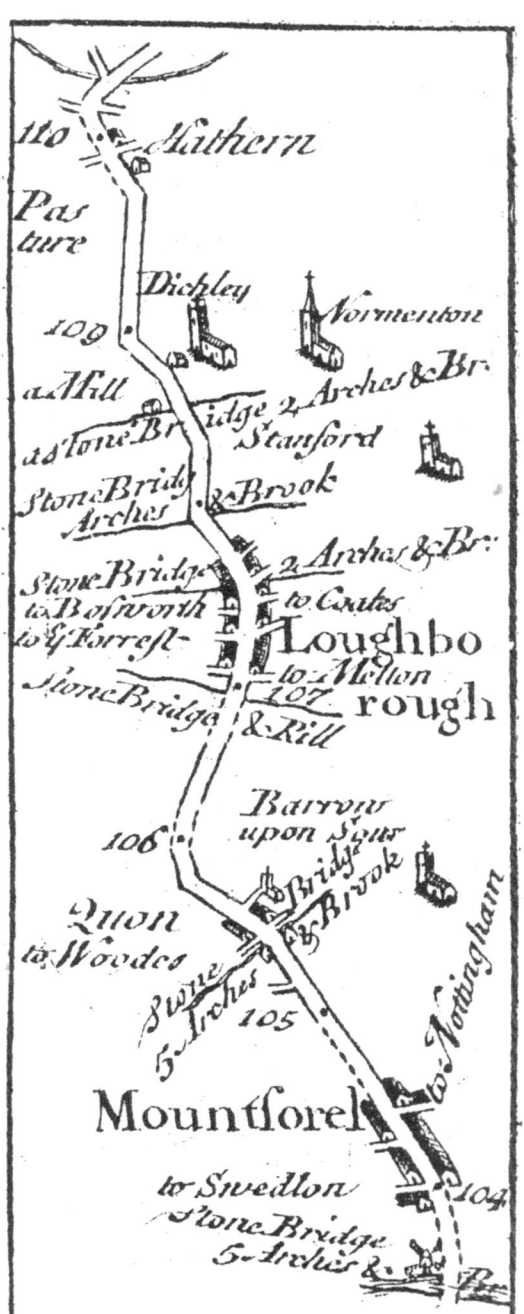

Part of a strip map from Britannia Depicta, *engraved by Emanuel Bowen in 1720, taken from Ogilby's maps of 1675. Bowen's maps were reproduced in the first pocket-size road atlas ever published, to be carried in large pockets by post boys who travelled the highways of England, delivering mail.*

A post boy on his horse in the 1670s, taken from an oil painting from this period.

A carrier's cart travelling between villages, selling goods to the local populace in the 18th century. This system of trade continued until World War Two in parts of Leicestershire.

This drawing shows the commonest form of travel for a family: a large shire horse fitted with two panniers. The squire, his lady and his daughter travel at a comfortable trot, possibly covering no more than 20 miles per day.

disrepair. From then until the end of the 18th century the main method of travel over long distances was on horseback. Because of the state of the roads, travel by coach was extremely uncomfortable and difficult, and above all it was expensive.

The main form of transport of goods for sale was through the system of packhorse and packhorse trains. Long lines of packhorses, comprising as many as 20 animals, were literally tied together 'tail by tail'. These trains travelled extremely long distances. Trackways for the transport of goods across Britain existed before the Roman occupation. Gold and salt from the Welsh mountains were carried to the North Sea during the Bronze Age period, in panniers on the back of packhorses.

The most efficient and quickest method of travel and carrying goods was by fast and reliable horses. In July 1635, Charles I ordered that a 'running post' must be positioned on all the main highways. Selected inns were chosen. These hostelries were enlarged to hold the change of horses, and there were approximately 70 miles between each post. The post boy would rest a while, refreshing himself with ale and bread and cheese, and then would be on his way again.

Large quantities of sheep and cattle would walk long distances accompanied by stockmen, or drovers, with their dogs. Drovers' track ways led to urban areas where large markets were held, such as at Spitalfields in London. Drove ways, or drifts, can still be found around Loughborough, and where the highway has not been widened, large areas of grassland still exist. As the animals travelled slowly along the highway, they grazed on these wide, grassed borders.

Horseback was the only method of travel across the open countryside, away from the main highways. Panniers could be fitted on large horses, allowing three people to be transported over long distances before the highways were improved to allow the passage of carts and coaches.

During the summer months it was possible to convey large quantities of goods by carrier cart, and this system gradually replaced the packhorse trains. Towards the end of the 17th century, through the development of the toll-gate system, the highways were repaired and maintained. The user paid for the use of the highway and this funded any maintenance.

King Charles II, after his coronation, made a series of decrees aimed at creating a better road system. The first Turnpike Act of 1663 authorised the setting up of toll gates, enabling a form of taxation to be levied locally. In Loughborough the responsibility for making up the roads was the duty of the civic controllers of the town. A coach trade slowly developed on the maintained toll roads. In 1784 John Palmer, the Controller-General of Post, set up the first mail coach run, and by 1790 mail coaches were operating all over Britain. The post boy on his horse was no longer required.

With the coming of the Industrial Revolution, the use of the highway changed. Towns such as Loughborough expanded enormously, especially through the development of the hosiery industry. In 1778 the canal system arrived in the town with the construction of the Soar Navigation. Heavy goods were now transported by water. Historically Loughborough was already an important town, the right to hold a Thursday market having been granted to Lord Beaumont during the reign of Edward II (1307–27), with annual fairs to be held on 1 August and 2 November. Once Loughborough was connected to the canal system, industry expanded. The town was altered further when the Midland Railway arrived, as goods, and eventually passengers, could travel directly to and from London after 1840. The Great Central Railway system opened in 1899 and closed in 1969. Today part of the Great Central Railway has been restored as a tourist feature and a working museum.

Today the modern highway has become the main method of transportation of goods and passengers, with freight carried by lorries and people by cars. The major road systems are part of modern history, with bypasses and dual carriageways forming part of the modern transport system. Future historians will no doubt comment on the changes that have taken place in this part of the East Midlands during the 20th and 21st century.

In this publication I have included a number of very fine drawings produced by William Edward Cooke. In 1877 he had a studio in Bowling Green Street, Leicester, and lived at Brook House, Quorn (a large Georgian house, now demolished). He moved to 21 Burton Street, Loughborough, Leicestershire in the 1880s, eventually living in Derby in the 1890s.

His drawings would have been produced from loose sketches or from a sketchbook by the artist. William Cooke was employed by Henry Wills as a commercial lithographic artist, and he would have completed commissioned work as required. All his printed drawings were drawn directly onto a polished lithographic stone or special zinc sheets. They were then printed and marketed by Henry Wills, bookseller, printer, bookbinder, lithographer and print frame maker, who also ran a circulating library from Nos 4 and 5 Market Place, Loughborough, Leicestershire.

An 18th-century wood engraving of a four-in-hand coach and horses. The coachman is sounding his horn as he arrives at his port of call. He would deliver parcels, mail and passengers, and change his horses.

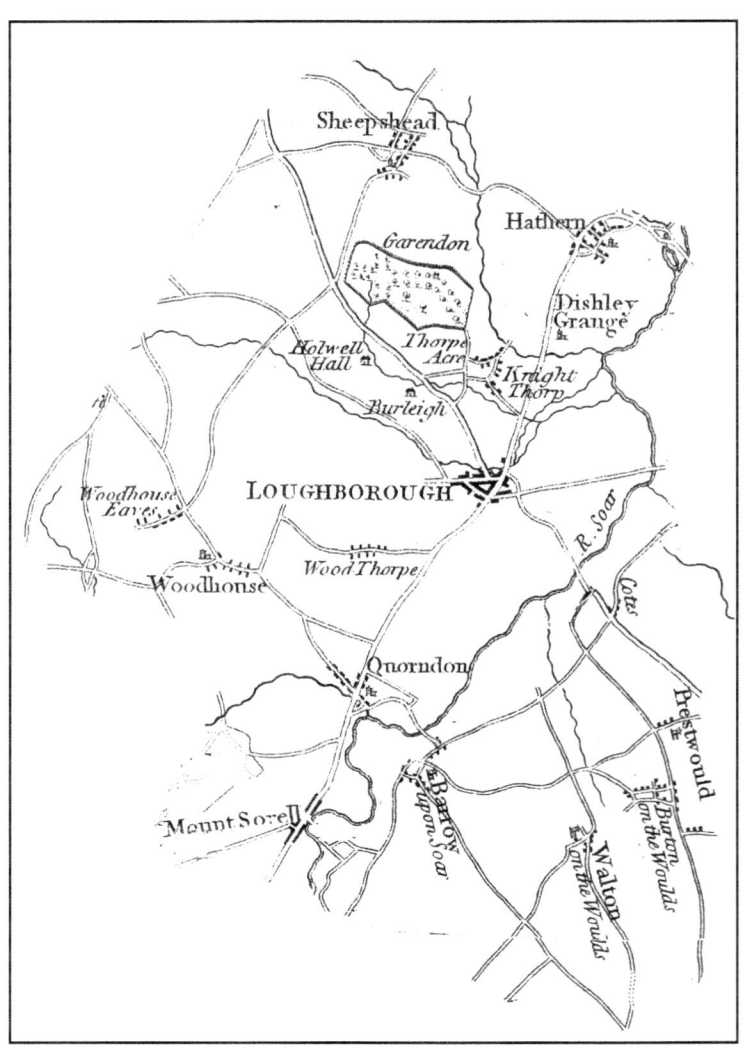

Two sections of two maps engraved by John Cary in 1800, featuring part of the West Goscote Hundred and the East Goscote Hundred. All the villages and the town of Loughborough featured in this book are listed.

Off The Salt Way

A trackway existed from Wales to the east coast of England during the Bronze Age, pre-dating the Roman occupation by 1,000 years. Tribes at that time traded with each other across what is now Europe and Scandinavia. Salt was a very important export and Welsh gold was desired throughout Northern Europe. There were many reasons for the Roman invasion of most of Great Britain, one of which is likely to have been the abundance of gold and other mined minerals in the islands.

Examining modern Ordnance Survey maps, it is easy to trace a line of roads in a reasonably straight route from Wales via Loughborough, picking up the drift road passing through Burton-on-the-Wolds. In Leicestershire this ancient road runs across the ridgeway out along the Vale of Belvoir escarpment and on to the flat lands of Lincolnshire.

The Romans must have used this trackway as a minor road linking Watling Street, the Fosse Way and Ermine Street. Even during the Danish occupation it was of importance, and it was a packhorse trail for over 1,000 years. In Burton-on-the-Wolds evidence of the trackway still exists, and a water fountain continually fills the horse trough with water.

In Cotes a 13-arch packhorse bridge formed a causeway crossing the River Soar and the marshes leading into Loughborough. It was a very important stone bridge connecting the west with the east on the Saxon/Danish highway. Originally the crossing was a ford and the first bridge, built of wood, was constructed before 1066. The hamlet of Cotes was created by King Ethelred (978–1016) as part of the parish of Prestwold.

During the Civil War an important battle took place at the bridge, on the Nottingham to Loughborough road. This was as a result of a skirmish on 16 March 1643 at Mountsorrel between Hastings's troops from Ashby de la Zouch and Roundheads from Leicester. Royalists were forced into a defensive position on Castle Hill in the village, from which they controlled the Loughborough road. They set up defensive earthworks at Cotes Bridge, which allowed the Royalists to control a considerable length of the important highway. After taking up their positions on 17 March, the two sides fought and skirmished for three days until the 20th.

Long-distance roads supported many markets, and a very important market was held at Walton-on-the-Wolds, just off the highway. There was also the famous Thursday market in Loughborough, and its two important fairs. Public houses served the coaching trade, and many still survive.

A photograph of Cotes water mill, off the Salt Way, c.1910.

Cotes

This engraving was published in 1793. It appears that the bridge consisted of 13 arches. The Soar was divided into four channels at this point. The bridge was half a mile in length and extremely narrow, a classic packhorse bridge. Supporting arches were built on three of the small islands standing on the flood plain. During the winter months, passage along the highway would not have been possible without this long bridge. Low supporting walls were constructed along the line of the causeway.

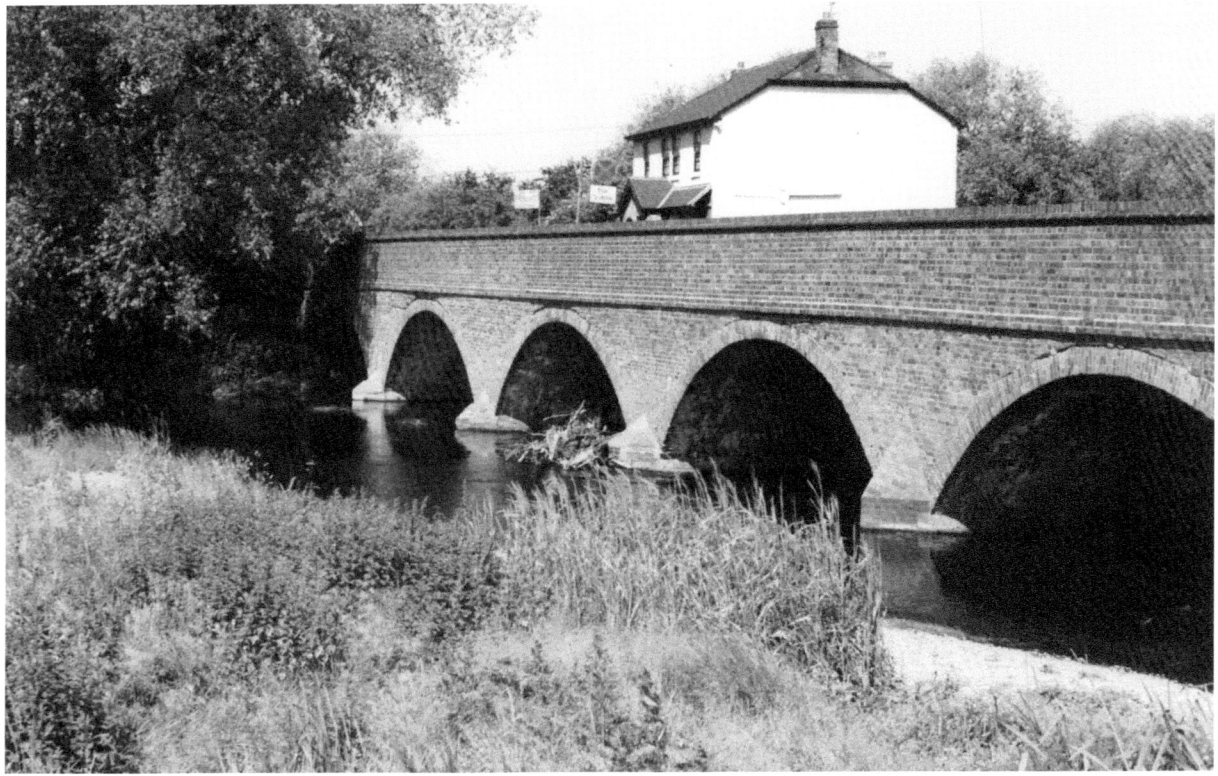

On the ancient highway now known as the A60 stands Cotes Bridge. In prehistoric times the River Soar would have been forded at the present site. The first bridge had probably been built of wood by 1066 to serve the two Saxon mills that had been erected nearby. In the small hamlet of Cotes, a church stands isolated in the fields.

Lower Cotes water mill in the 1930s. It was still grinding corn for bread flour in 1950, but by 1951 it was only grinding animal food. The mill ceased working in 1973 and was the last working water mill in Leicestershire at that time.

Upper Cotes water mill in 1890. It was possibly destroyed when the walls of the mill pond were blown up to relieve local flooding on the River Soar.

A drawing produced by William Edward Cooke in 1888, of Lower Cotes water mill. The artist lived at 21 Burton Street, Loughborough in the 1880s and moved to Derby in the 1890s.

The remains of one of the two 18ft diameter waterwheels still standing at the water mill at Cotes in 2003.

The preserved sack hoist at Cotes Water mill in 2003.

The fast-flowing River Soar at Cotes Bridge in 1991. There is evidence that some of the ancient stone bridge has been retained in the modern structure. The remains of a weir are still visible.

The author with Jo Humberston inside Lower Cotes water mill, now a pleasant restaurant, in 2004.

The mill pond at Lower Cotes water mill in 2003.

The River Soar leaving Lower Cotes water mill, looking towards the weir, before World War One.

A section of Cotes Bridge, with the mill stream leaving the water mill, in 1880.

Prestwold

An engraving by J.P. Malcolm of the Church of St Andrew at Prestwold in 1792.

Prestwold church, 2007. A mediaeval church with a Perpendicular west tower, constructed sometime after 1350 and before 1500. Considerable rebuilding took place in 1890. In the church there are numerous memorials to the Packe family.

The lodge gates to Prestwold Hall, seen in a photograph taken in the 1920s. The neo-Greek porticoes were possibly built in 1821.

The Church of St Andrew and Prestwold Hall in 1988. The deserted village would have stood on the grassed area in front of the church and hall, and may have been destroyed in the 14th century when the hall was erected in support of the expanding sheep trade.

Prestwold Hall in the summer of 2007. The church and hall are now used for weddings. It is a beautiful venue, with the marriage taking place in the church, followed by a picturesque journey to a reception in the historic hall.

Prestwold Hall in an engraving by W. Radclyffe from a drawing by J.P. Neale, published in London in 1829.

A very fine photograph of Prestwold Hall, taken in the 1920s.

An engraving produced by William Walter in 1791, showing the home of Charles James Packe. A fine memorial has been erected in St Andrew's Church in his memory, dated 1839.

Burton-on-the-Wolds

The fountain at Burton-on-the-Wolds, drawn by William Edward Cooke in 1880. Water rises from an artesian well, brought to the surface through underground pressure via a fracture in the rock.

The fountain at Burton-on-the-Wolds in 2009. It was constructed to provide water on the Salt Way and may have existed for over 1,000 years. How many people and horses have quenched their thirst at this trough? Today cyclists still take a drink as they pass.

The Greyhound Inn on Melton Road, Burton-on-the-Wolds, 2006. An 18th-century public house, it originally served the coaching trade along the Salt Way. In 1862 William Chamberlain was a carrier based at this inn, trading into the Thursday market at Loughborough. The landlord of the inn in 1846 was Anthony Hart, in 1862 it was Richard Grundy, and in 1877 William Tuckwood and his wife took over. They were landlords into the early 1900s. They had the right to graze the wide, grassed highway along the Salt Way, which was normally allocated by election through the village council.

The entrance to Prestwold Hall. Built in 1740, it was extensively altered as a hunting lodge in the 1790s and altered again in the early part of the 20th century. At the end of the 19th century it was the home of Lord Archibald Henry Algernon St Maur.

A general view of the village of Walton-on-the-Wolds in about 1900.

The small village green in the centre of Walton-on-the-Wolds, c.1900. The market cross may have stood in this area of the village in the 18th century.

The Anchor Inn, Walton-on-the-Wolds, 2006. There is evidence that it was involved in the coaching trade and supporting the local markets. In 1846 Henry Holmes was the landlord and in 1863 Ann Rouse ran the pub. In 1877, Arthur Thomas Smith was the publican and also a wheelwright, repairing wheels from the carrier carts of the Salt Way. He was still running the hostelry in 1880. William Brown took over in the 1890s, maintaining a carrier's cart transporting goods to the Thursday and Saturday markets at Loughborough well into the early part of the 20th century.

A photograph of the Rectory at Walton-on-the-Wolds, c.1920. In 1922 Revd Montague Bertie Bird BA lived in this house and was the vicar of the Church of St Mary.

The Church of St Mary in 2006. This church has a very chequered history. In 1736 the mediaeval church was pulled down on the instruction of the churchwardens and village constables, to be rebuilt in brick. The incumbent, Revd Augustus Packe (of Prestwold Hall), financed the construction of the chancel from preserved stone in the Gothic style. In 1846 Revd Augustus Hobart MA was vicar, and in 1863 Revd George Trevor Spencer DD was rector. In 1877 Revd John Bird MA was appointed vicar and he held this position well into the 20th century. In 1877 he financed the construction of the nave in the church.

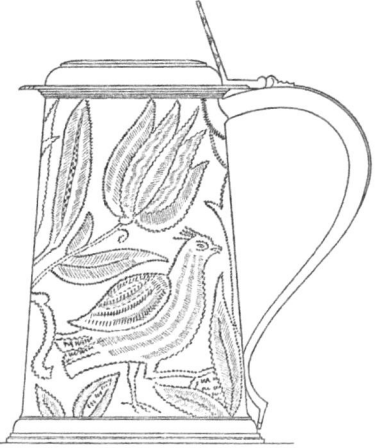

A pewter flagon that was presented to the mediaeval church in about 1700. On the top and under the lid are star and lozenge shapes. On the base of the flagon, flowers, leaves and two large birds have been engraved in a series of dots.

An engraving of the Church of St Mary in 1800. Interestingly, the market cross stands in front of the brick-built building.

The remains of the market cross standing in the churchyard in Walton-on-the-Wolds in 1800. It is recorded that the original mediaeval structure of the church was demolished prior to 1736 and rebuilt in brick. It is presumed that in about 1740 the market cross was removed from the centre of the village on the instructions of the village constable and erected on its existing site. The packhorse trade supporting the village market had virtually disappeared by that period and carriers' carts had taken over, based at the local hostelry.

The famous market cross in 2009, its restoration evident when compared with the 1800 engraving. On its original site in the centre of the village it marked the place where the people living in and around the village would hold their weekly market. Some markets dated back to before the Roman occupation, and they were a feature of religious law after the Norman occupation, when the Church and State controlled all village markets. In the 1360s King Edward III granted markets to lords of the manor. Markets such as the one at Walton-on-the-Wolds were then controlled by the Church.

Loughborough

Loughborough is a market town of considerable importance and the largest town in Leicestershire. John Leland (c.1506–1552) described it as: 'Yn Largeness and good building, next to Leyrcester, of all the markette townes yn the shire', in around 1540. Historically, the market is held on Thursdays. The street market was granted by Edward II (1307–24) to Lady Beaumont, who also had the right to hold fairs on 28 March, 25 April, Holy Thursday, as close as possible to 12 August and 13 November. These were open markets for the sale of horses, cattle and sheep. On 30 September and 24 March there were fairs to sell Leicestershire cheese.

Loughborough was considered to be a village during the Saxon period, and when John Prior of Ashby de la Zouch published his map in 1777 it was just a collection of houses on an important road junction. The canal that became the Grand Union Canal had reached Loughborough, but the 'cut' had yet to be undertaken south-east of the town. The Industrial Revolution changed everything. Industry expanded, particularly hosiery and heavy industry, with the casting of bells from 1858. In 1909 the Technical Institute was founded, which eventually developed into Loughborough University. In the following pages numerous advertisements, published in the 19th century, are featured, with particular emphasis on the market square.

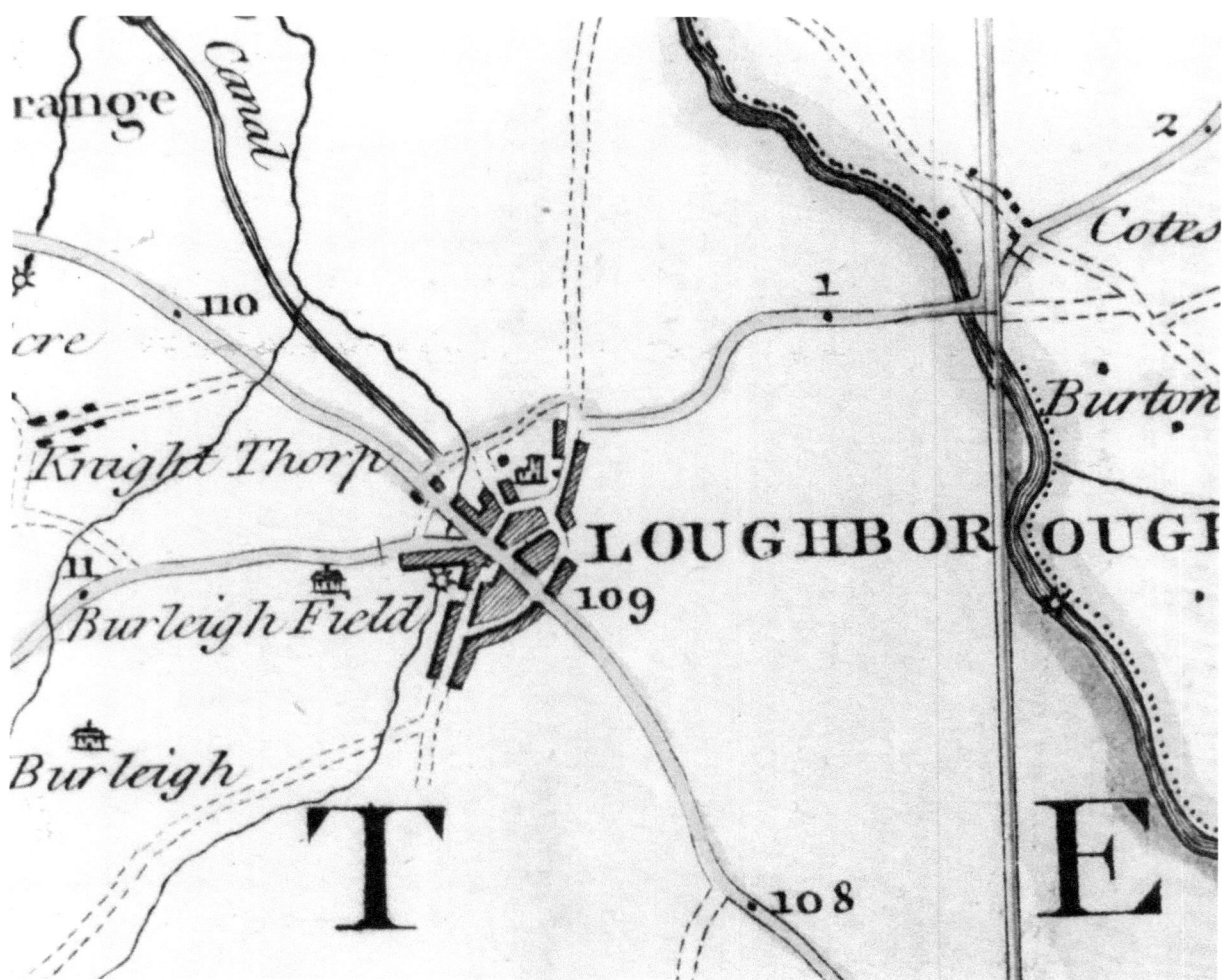

A section from John Prior's map of 1777. The canal had just reached the town of Loughborough. The Salt Way goes straight through the town.

A view of Loughborough published in 1789, from an engraving by William Walker. In the foreground stands a windmill. This post mill was still standing in 1836. The Church of All Saints stands high in the background.

All Saints' Church, Loughborough, an engraving of the north-west view, c.1790.

A silver cup with cover paten, donated to All Saints' Church. The design and engraving suggest it could have been made in around 1610. Under the foot the weight is inscribed: '13ozs.15ducts'.

A fine engraving of the north view of All Saints' Church, Loughborough, c.1790.

The interior of All Saints' Church, c.1905.

The home of the vicar of All Saints' Church, Revd Francis Wilcox, in 1797.

All Saints' Church in 1905. The vicar was Revd Thomas Pitts MA. A 14th-century building, it was extensively restored in 1860–63.

All Saints' Church in 2002.

EMMANUEL DYBALL,

ROYAL OAK INN,

LEICESTER ROAD,

LOUGHBOROUGH.

CHOICE WINES, SPIRITS, AND CIGARS.

SPLENDID DRAUGHT AND BOTTLE ALES, PORTER, &c., &c.

An advertisement by Emmanuel Dyball, the landlord of the Royal Oak Inn on Leicester Road, Loughborough, in 1877.

The Royal Oak Inn on Leicester Road, Loughborough, in 1904 when the landlord was John Dyball.

The Royal Oak on Leicester Road, Loughborough, in 2009.

HENRY ASTILL,

WOOLSTAPLER,

AND

ALE & PORTER MERCHANT,

BAXTER GATE, LOUGHBOROUGH.

Truman, Hanbury, Buxton, & Co.'s London Porter and Brown Stout, in 18-Gallon Casks and upwards, also in Pint & Quarter Bottles.

SAMUEL ALLSOPP & SON'S

Burton Ales & East India Pale Ale,

From 8d. per Gallon up to 2s. Ditto.

EAST INDIA PALE ALE, in Pint & Quart Bottles, SPLENDID STRONG BOTTLED ALES, ALWAYS IN PRIME CONDITION.

Agent to the Equitable Fire & National Loan Fund Life Offices.

An interesting advertisement from 1853. It would be remarkable if Henry Astill did not supply ale to the Royal Oak Inn.

CORNELIUS WOODING,
BOOKSELLER & NEWS AGENT,
TOBACCONIST, & BILL POSTER,
Church Gate, Loughborough.

C. WOODING begs most respectfully to return his best thanks to the Inhabitants of Loughborough and its Neigbourhood, for the very liberal support they have bestowed upon him during the time he has been in business, and to assure them that nothing on his part shall be wanting to merit a continuance of their kind patronage. He also informs them that he has made arrangements whereby he is enabled to supply all the LONDON WEEKLY & MONTHLY NEWSPAPERS, and PUBLICATIONS, as soon as published.

AGENT FOR LEWIS'S CONCENTRATED PURATIVE PILLS,
Silver Cream, Balsamic Ointment, Electerium, &c.
DAIRDSON'S MUSICAL TREASURY AND BOUQUETS.
Nottingham Review, Nottinghamshire Guardian, Penny Railway Time Tables, &c. &c.

A fascinating advertisement published in 1853. Cornelius Wooding sold concentrated purative pills along with newspapers and magazines!

A busy market day in Loughborough in 2002. You would get a strange look if you went into any of the shops on this highway and asked for purative pills.

SUTHERLAND HOUSE,

VICTORIA ROAD, LOUGHBOROUGH.

Only a Limited Number of YOUNG LADIES received.

———◦◦◦◦———

THE course of STUDY comprises the subjects required for the Cambridge Local Examinations, and the several branches of a liberal ENGLISH EDUCATION, together with FRENCH, GERMAN, MUSIC, DRAWING, and PAINTING, in WATER COLOURS, by good Masters.

The French Language is Spoken Daily, with a resident French Lady.

MRS. GAULTIER

Has had great experience in Tuition as Private Governess in Families of Rank.

———◦◦◦———

Sutherland House is Large, Healthy, and Pleasantly Situated, in the best part of Loughborough.

Sutherland House, Victoria Road, Loughborough, 1877.

Sutherland House, now Bedford House, 16 Victoria Street, 2009.

Leicester Road, Loughborough, c.1900. Sutherland House was located just off the main road to the left of the photograph.

An extremely fine drawing by William Edward Cooke, 1880. These shops stood in the Market Place, Loughborough, and were demolished in 1887. Constantine Dufner, Jeweller and Watchmaker, stood at 33 Market Place, while Henry Matthews, butchers, was at 34 Market Place.

An advertisement for Henry Wills's shop at 4 Market Place, Loughborough, in 1880. The printing workshop was at Angel Yard. The firm eventually became Wills and Hepworth, the fine printer and publisher of Ladybird Books. William Edward Cooke worked for Henry Wills for many years, and the drawing of the bridge on a river used in this advertisement was produced by Cooke.

A view of the Market Place, Loughborough, c.1900.

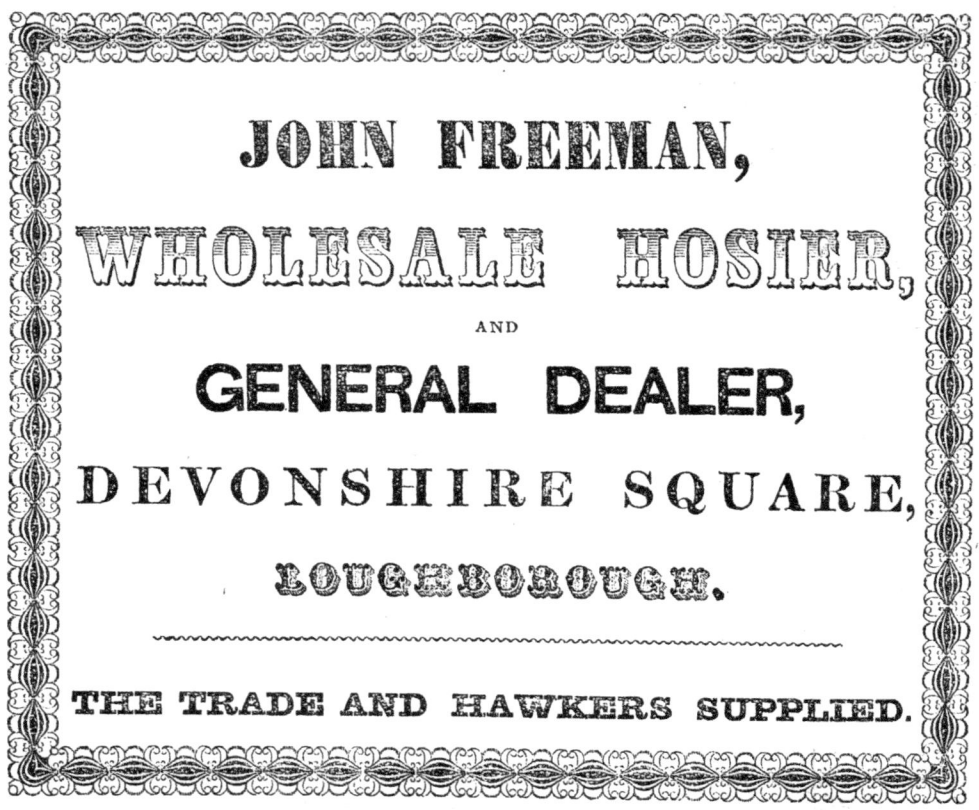

JOHN FREEMAN,
WHOLESALE HOSIER,
AND
GENERAL DEALER,
DEVONSHIRE SQUARE,
LOUGHBOROUGH.
THE TRADE AND HAWKERS SUPPLIED.

An advertisement for a dealer in hosiery in 1853 off Devonshire Square, Loughborough.

CURZON
W.I. MARKETS

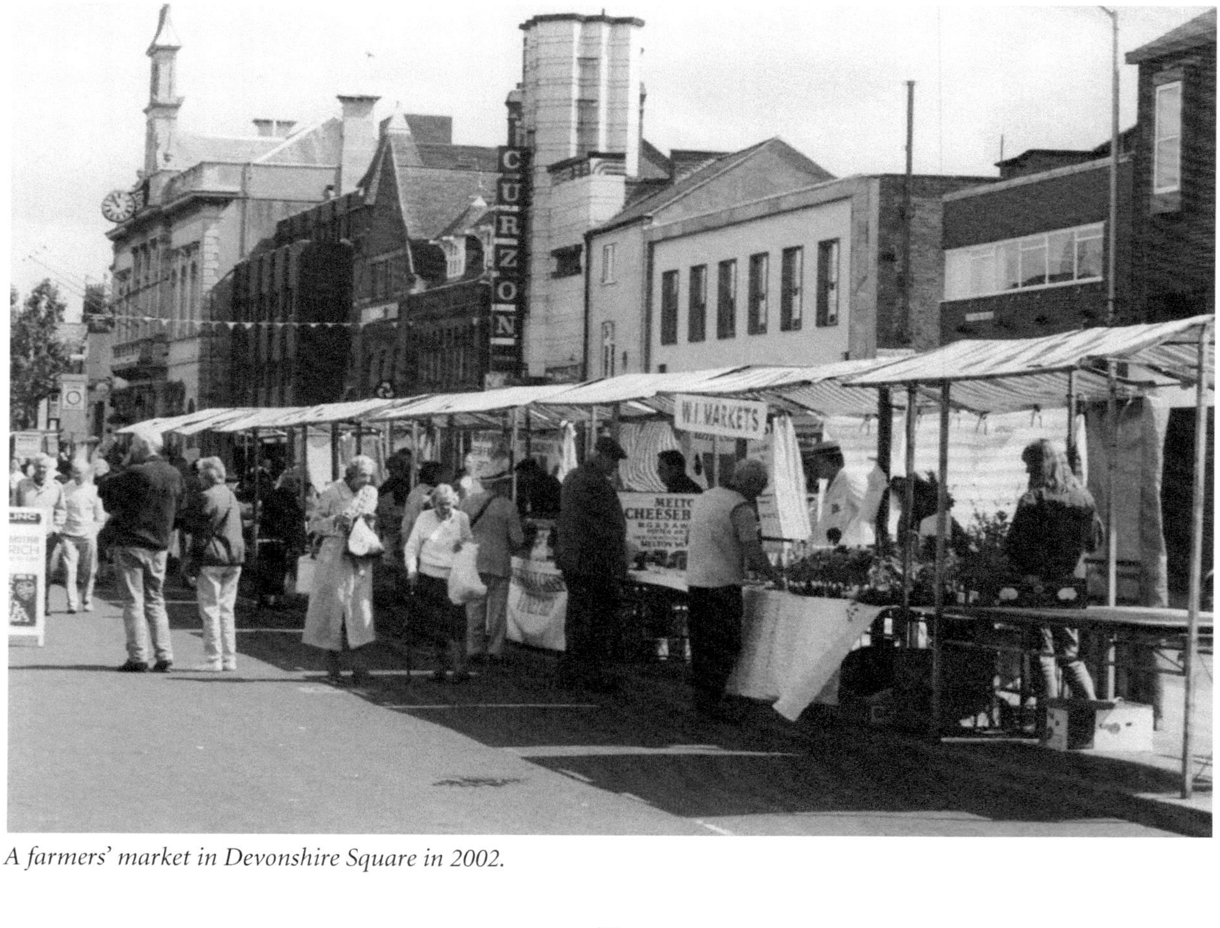

A farmers' market in Devonshire Square in 2002.

The Thursday market, looking towards the Town Hall, in 2002.

A very interesting 1905 photograph of the Thursday market in progress, with the Lord Nelson public house dominating the Market Square. The landlord at the time was James Gutteridge, and he ran the pub through the years of World War One.

The Market Place, Loughborough, c.1910.

Another 1910 view of the Market Place, Loughborough.

The Market Place, Loughborough c.1910.

The Market Place, Loughborough, in 1912. The Town Hall is in the background and T.F. Keightly's ironmonger's shop can also be seen.

The Market Place, Loughborough, c.1930.

The market in full swing in Loughborough on a Thursday in the late 1920s or early 1930s.

The Thursday market at Loughborough in 2002 with The Sock *sculpture visible. Hosiery was one of the main sources of income to the town in the 19th and early 20th century.*

The Market Place, Loughborough, in 1922. James Gutteridge is still the licensee of the Lord Nelson public house. In the centre background is Arthur Martin's chemist shop at 22 Market Place, situated next to Lewis Start's Tobacconists at No. 23.

An isolated market stall in the Market Place, Loughborough, c.1900, with the Town Hall in the background.

Church Gate, Loughborough, c.1910.

JOSEPH GRIGGS & CO., L<u>TD.</u>,

... IMPORTERS OF ...

FOREIGN WOOD GOODS,

— AND —

BUILDING MATERIAL MERCHANTS.

Chief Office: Loughborough, Leicestershire.

FOREIGN WOOD GOODS

. . IMPORTED INTO . .

WEST HARTLEPOOL, HULL, LONDON, CARDIFF, FELIXSTOWE AND MANCHESTER;

Other Depots: Gloucester, Liverpool and Barrow-in-Furness.

The following descriptions of Wood Goods always in Stock :

Archangel, Petersburg, Gefle, Soderham, Bjorneborg, Wyburg and Riga Red and White Deals, Battens and Boards ; Quebec Yellow and Pitch Pine and Spruce Deals ; also Flooring, Matched Boards, Mouldings and Manufactured Joinery ; Slaters' and Plasterers' Laths.

Importers of the ♛ C. R. W. ♛ and J. S. & CO., and other Patent Laths.

BUILDING MATERIALS.

The following supplied at Lowest Market Prices :

Roofing Slates : — Penrhyn, Dinorwic, Velenheli, Carnarvon, Portmadoc and all other Welsh Slates. Westmorland, Whitland Abbey and Delabole Green Slates, and Burlington Dark Round Heads.

Patent Slate Ridging, Slate Slabs, Cisterns, &c. Staffordshire and Broseley Roofing Tiles, Ridge Tiles, Quarries, Garden Tiles, &c.

Blue, Red and White Building and Paving Bricks and Fire Bricks.

Bridgwater Roman Tiles ; Norfolk Red and Phillips' Patent Lock-jaw Tiles.

Glazed Sanitary Pipes, Chimney Tops and Sanitary Goods of all descriptions.

York Stone from all Quarries ; also Mansfield, Ackworth, Ancaster, Hollington, Darley Dale, Alton, Bromsgrove and Corsham Bath Stone.

Mountsorrel, Enderby and Charnwood Granite. Portland and Roman Cement, Lime and Plaster of all kinds.

TELEGRAMS: "GRIGGS, LOUGHBOROUGH."

Estimates given for every class of Building Materials for Home & Export Trade.

A very descriptive advertisement covering a wide range of imports into Loughborough, between the years 1891 and 1899.

Brush Electrical Engineering Works, Loughborough, c.1900.

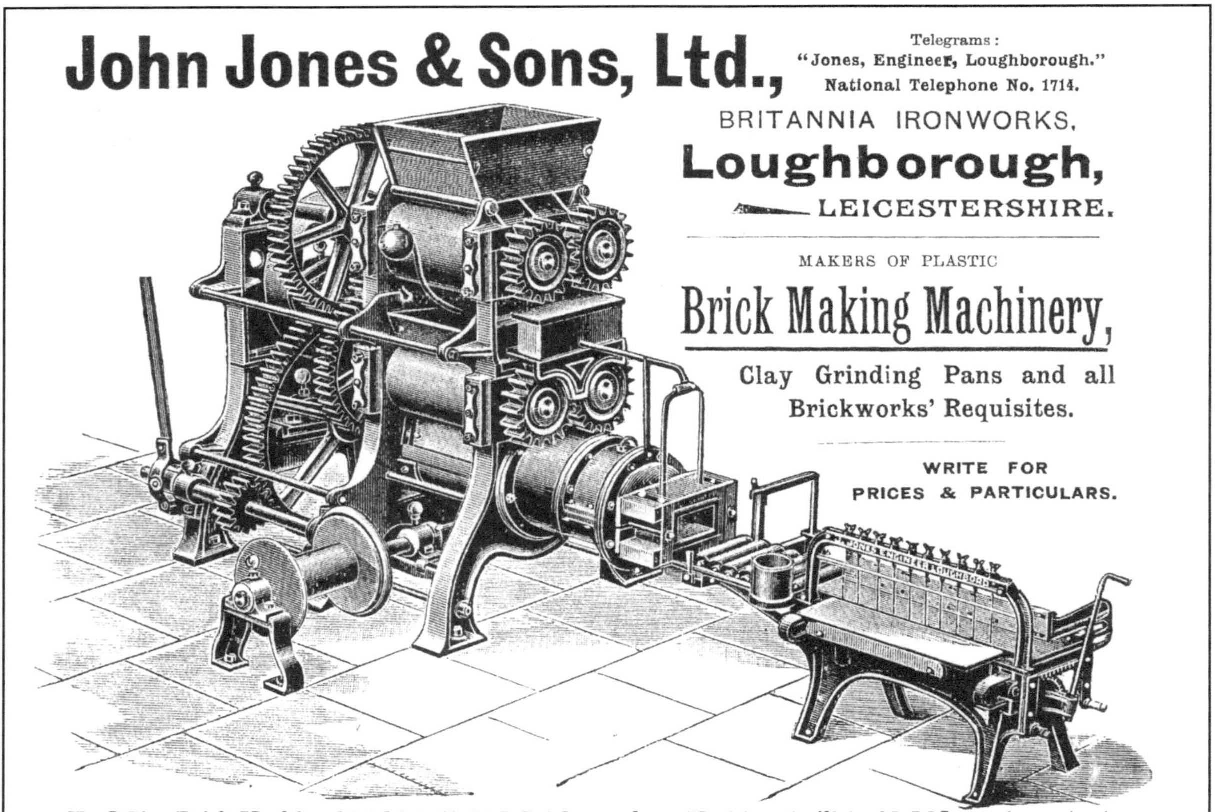

John Jones & Sons, Ltd.,

Telegrams :
"Jones, Engineer, Loughborough."
National Telephone No. 1714.

BRITANNIA IRONWORKS,

Loughborough,

— LEICESTERSHIRE.

MAKERS OF PLASTIC

Brick Making Machinery,

Clay Grinding Pans and all
Brickworks' Requisites.

**WRITE FOR
PRICES & PARTICULARS.**

No. 2 Size Brick Machine, 10,000 to 12,000 Bricks per day. Machines built to 40,000 per day output.

This advertisement was for the Britannia Ironworks at Loughborough during the years 1899 to 1904.

The Brush Electrical Engineering Works at Loughborough, c.1910.

SAMUEL FRISBY & SON,

General Ironmongers,

BAR IRON MERCHANTS

IRON AND BRASS FOUNDERS,

BRAZIERS,

IRON, ZINC, & TIN PLATE WORKERS,

MARKET PLACE,

LOUGHBOROUGH.

An advertisement for Samuel Frisby & Son's iron and brass founders workshop, 1853.

An oil painting of the Town Hall in the centre of Loughborough, 1905. The hall was built in 1855 by William States as the Corn Exchange.

Two photographs of the Thursday market outside the Town Hall, Loughborough, in 2002.

A meet of the Quorn Hounds in the Market Place, Loughborough, Bank Holiday Monday, January 1911. James Gutteridge was licensee of the Lord Nelson public house and served the 'stirrup cup' to the Master of the Quorn Hunt, Captain Frank Forester, and his guests.

Forest Road, Loughborough, in the 1930s.

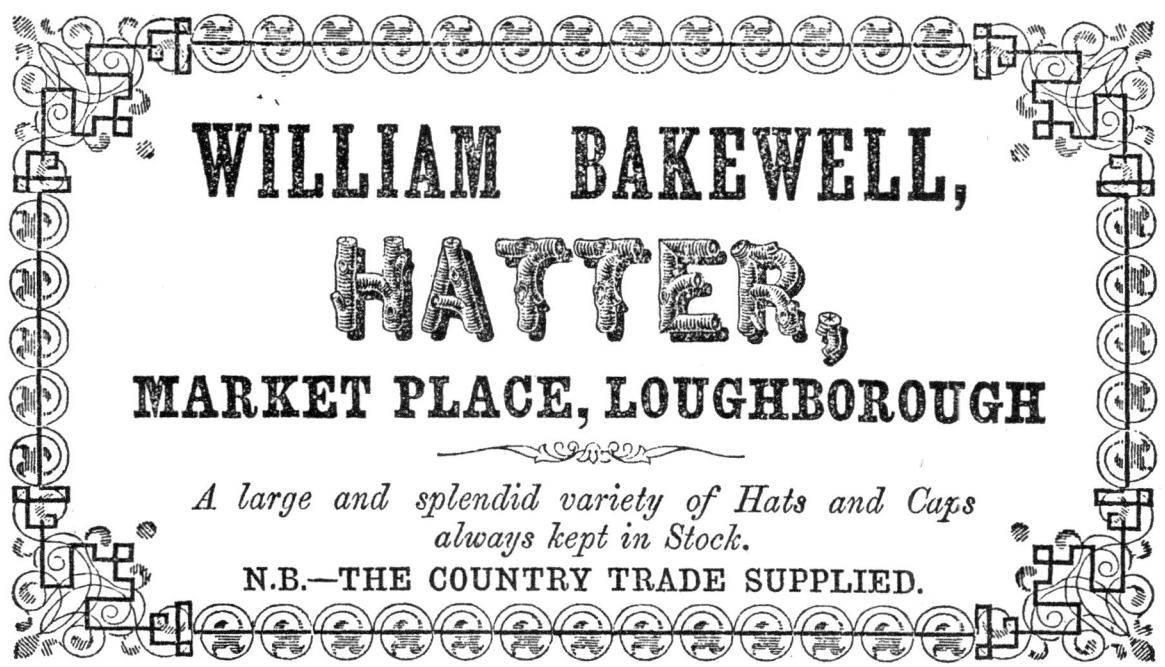

William Bakewell supplied hunting caps to the Quorn Hunt.

An engraving of the Free Grammar School, Loughborough, from 1852, the year it was built by a local mason, Thomas Walpole.

The Grammar School at Loughborough, 1905.

The Carnegie Library, 1912.

The Carnegie Library, built 1903–05, in a contemporary photograph. It was constructed by Barrowcliff & Allcock.

Queen's Park, Loughborough, 1905.

The bridge in Queen's Park, Loughborough, c.1930.

The Band Stand in Queen's Park, Loughborough, 1905.

The Carillon Tower in Queen's Park, Loughborough, built 1922–23 by Walter Tappier. It was constructed with a belvedere top and copper roof. It is 151ft high and holds 47 bells. The building was dedicated to those who lost their lives in World War One. This is a contemporary photograph. The tower now also carries a World War Two dedication.

The lake in Queen's Park, Loughborough, c.1905.

The front of Charnwood Museum in Queen's Park on Granby Street, Loughborough, 2002. It is one of the best small museums in Loughborough and is a very fine educational facility with many good exhibits. Opened as a museum on 10 August 1998, it was originally built as the town's baths in 1897.

An Auster aeroplane suspended from the ceiling in the Charnwood Museum, Loughborough. This plane was made by Auster Aircraft Ltd at the village of Rearsby in 1947. It was one of 3,800 such planes that were built from 1939–1968, principally for the army. This plane is G-AJRH, winner of the 1956 King's Cup air race.

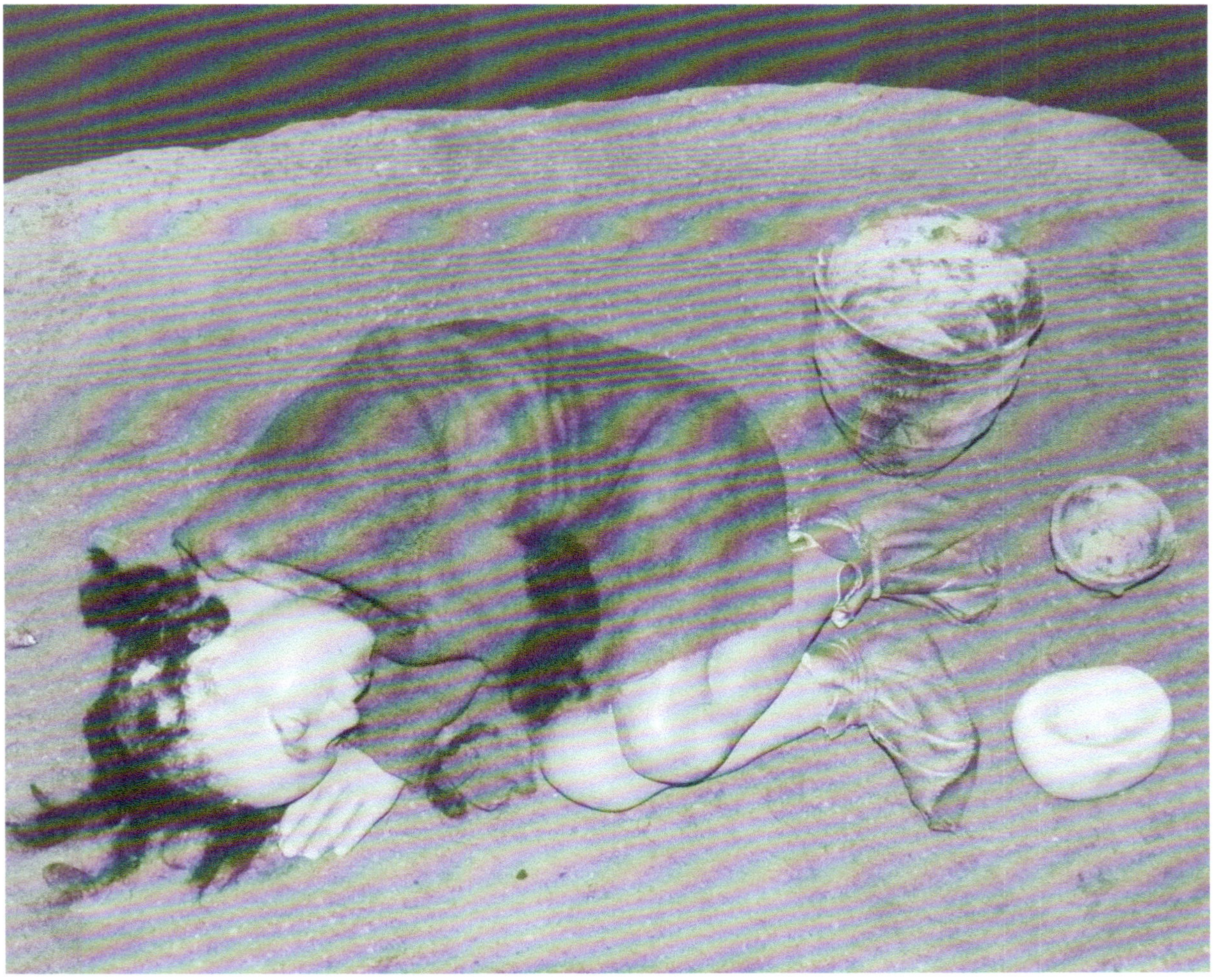

A Bronze Age burial on display in the Charnwood Museum, Loughborough, 2002. This is a reconstruction of a grave found near Cossington on an archaeological dig. It shows the remains of an eight-year-old boy who died nearly 4,000 years ago. It is presumed that this is how he was clothed when his body was buried. Pottery vessels and implements were placed with the body, as they were considered essential in the afterlife.

A display constructed in Charnwood Museum, Loughborough, 2002. Dig for Victory! Land Army girls worked on the land during World War Two.

J. G. CAYLESS & SONS,

MIDLAND

𝔑et, 𝔗ent, & 𝔚aterproof 𝔠loth 𝔚orks,

ROPE, TWINE, AND SACK MANUFACTORY,

LOUGHBOROUGH.

TENTS AND MARQUEES FOR HIRE.

An 1877 advertisement. How much of Cayless's cloth was used as protection in the Loughborough market?

Loughborough market at the turn of the 20th century.

Wright's Mill in Market Street, the site of John Heathcote's factory in the 1980s. Formerly Mill Street, Market Street was the site of the only major skirmish involving Luddite workers in the 18th and 19th century in Leicestershire. On 28 June 1816 a mob of 100 men with blackened faces charged down Mill Street and smashed their way into John Heathcote's lace factory, armed with pistols. They shot and wounded one of the armed factory watchmen, John Asher; nine others surrendered. The men then destroyed all the lacemaking machines. Eventually eight men from the mob were apprehended. Their leader James Towle and four others were hanged at Leicester gaol in April 1817; the remaining three were transported. Heathcote sold up and set up his business in Devon.

Market Street, Loughborough, 2003.

The Grand Union Canal, Loughborough, c.1910.

The weir near Loughborough controlling the flow of the River Soar into the Grand Union Cana', c.1910.

The locks on the Grand Union Canal near Belton Road, Loughborough, 2009.

Bridge 41 on the Grand Union Canal, on Swing Bridge Road, Loughborough, 2009.

A barge passing through the locks on the Grand Union Canal near Belton Road, Loughborough, 2009.

Bridgeside Cottages, built on the site of the wharf in Loughborough, on a short length of canal leading off the Grand Union Canal.

The Bull's Head Hotel sign displayed across High Street in 1904. The landlord was Edwin Lewis Meadows. Signs such as this have their origins in gibbets erected across the road. Highway robbers, especially those who had stolen the king's post, were hung up on display as a deterrent to others.

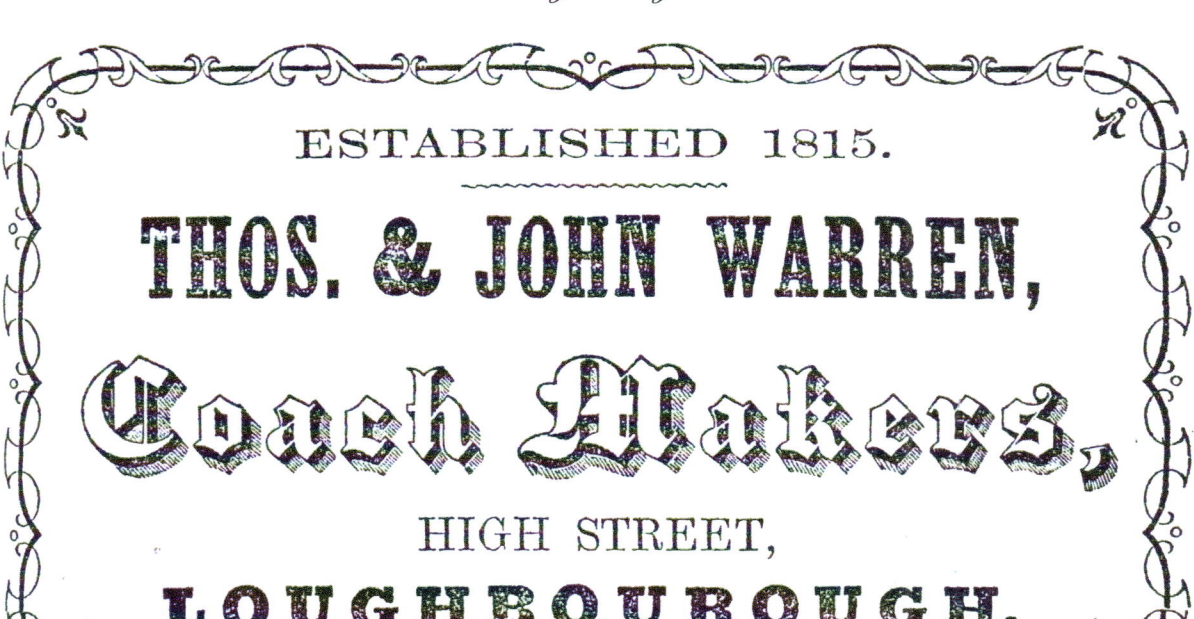

ESTABLISHED 1815.
THOS. & JOHN WARREN,
Coach Makers,
HIGH STREET,
LOUGHBOUROUGH.

An 1853 advertisement. This workshop was close to the Bull's Head Hotel.

CROWN & CUSHION
LOUGHBOROUGH
CROWN & CUSHION
CROWN & CUSHION
CAR PARK

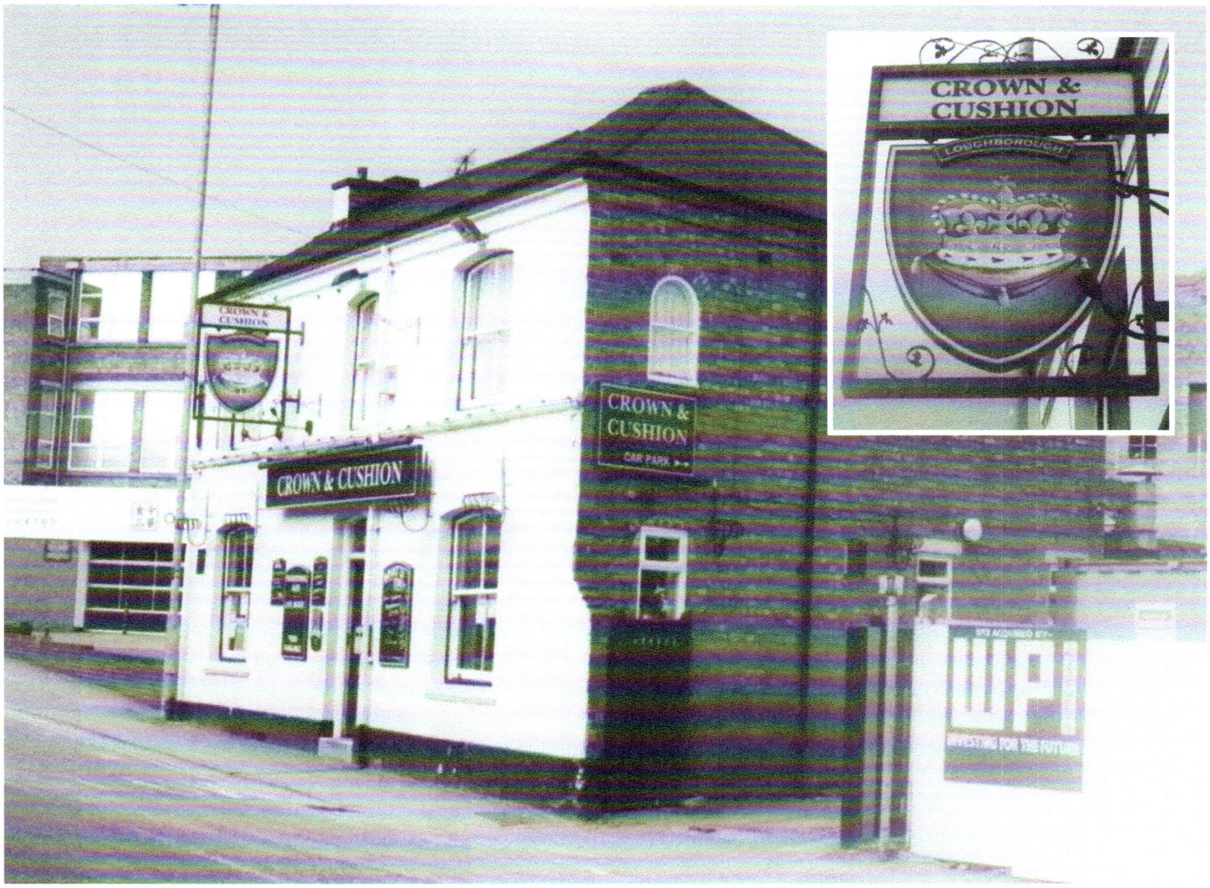

The Crown and Cushion public house in 2009. It is an inn that is steeped in history, situated off Ashby Square, Loughborough. From the 1870s through to the turn of the 20th century John Thomas Fisher wcs the licensee, and from 1900 to 1928 William Orm was the landlord.

The Old Pack Horse Inn, 2009. A hostelry such as this might have existed on the Salt Road that passed through Loughborough for 1,000 years. The landlords are well documented: 1846 Jonathan Waterfield, 1862 William Yates, 1886 Mrs Harriet Bennington, 1899 William Tristam Richardson, 1904 Matthew Maile Johnson. After World War One the landlord was William Sheffield.

The Swan in the Rushes in 2009. The pub has changed names over the past 100 years.

'The Griffin'.

The Griffin, off Ashby Square, Loughborough, 2009. The griffin was a mythological creature consisting of an eagle on a lion's body. In the 19th century the pub had numerous landlords: 1846 William Rowarth, 1862 Henry Harridge, 1877–1890s George Wither, 1893 John Chambers, 1899 John Sherlock and then, at the turn of the 20th century, John Alfred Geary.

The Great Central Railway

The Great Central Hotel, Loughborough, c.1910. It is situated near to the Great Central Railway Station. In 1940 Joseph Arthur Frake was the owner.

Station Hotel, Dalby Road, Loughborough, 2009. A magnificent Victorian building, its owner in 1899 was Walter Bastow, and by 1928 it belonged to Arthur Gordon Yeomans.

The Great Central Railway Station, Loughborough, which opened in 1899. This is the entrance and ticket room as seen in 2002. It is possible to take a trip into the past by walking along the Edwardian platform and taking a short train journey on a steam train.

A 20th-century ticket issued in the 21st century, as part of the working museum's nostalgic train travel experience.

> GREAT CENTRAL RAILWAY
> 1st CLASS
> **DAY RUNABOUT TICKET**
> Between
> **Loughborough (Central)**
> and
> **LEICESTER NORTH**
> VALID ON DAY OF ISSUE ONLY. FOR CONDITIONS SEE OVER.

W.H. Smith & Son on the platform of the Great Central Railway in 2009. All railway stations had W.H. Smith's kiosks to this traditional design.

British Rail engine No.90775 leaving the Great Central Station on the way to Quorn & Woodhouse, Rothley and Leicester North Station, 2002.

Steaming out of the Great Central Railway Station, 2002.

British Rail engine No.78019, in steam, about to leave the Great Central Station, 2009.

The sidings on the Great Central Railway at Loughborough, 2009. In the centre background is tne station, with the water tower adjacent to the footpath.

Skilful engineers repairing a firebox and boiler at the locomotive sheds outside the Great Central Workshops at Loughborough, 2009.

Rothley Station on the Great Central Railway, 2009.

Boarding the first-class dining car at the Great Central Railway, 2009.

Lorna Maybery enjoying an evening meal in the first-class
dining car on the Great Central Railway, 2002.

Amy Grech enjoying a midday meal in the first-class
dining car on the Great Cent-al Railway, 2009.

The Bells

The bell 'Great Paul' leaving Loughborough for St Paul's Cathedral, London, May 1882. The Taylor family were running a bell foundry in St Neots, Huntingdonshire, by 1786. The family moved to Loughborough in 1828 to start casting bells in this world-famous foundry.

A parade of bells leaving Taylor's bell foundry in 1922 to be hung in the Carillon Tower in Queen's Park, Loughborough.

A bell hanging in Taylor's foundry. The men are checking the swing, March 1882.

Boring for the clapper-bolt from the inside of the bell, April 1882.

Positioning the bell for the first testing for tone, March 1882.

Boring for the clapper-bolt from the outside of the bell, April 1882.

A carillon of bells being constructed at Taylor's foundry, Loughborough, in 2002.

The carillon of bells being assembled at Taylor's foundry to be positioned in the Carillon Tower on Queen's Park, Loughborough, 1922.

Some 47 bells were dedicated by people and organisations, then cast at Taylor's foundry to be hung in the Loughborough Carillon. This bell records Peter Sellars, of the 6th Leicestershire Regiment.

Taylor's foundry in 2002.

Casting bell crowns in Taylor's foundry, Loughborough, June 2002.

Taylor's bell foundry in Freehold Street, Loughborough, is the largest bell foundry in the world.

A selection of bells with new castings and very old bells that have been returned for re-tuning at Taylor's bell foundry, 2002.

Bells being tuned at Taylor's foundry, 2002. Bells produce more than one note when struck, but the overall sound should harmonise.

The Soar Valley

The Soar Valley is steeped in history, and its important road is now the A6. The River Soar is connected with the River Trent and thus the sea, and it is possible that the Vikings/Danes came down this river in the eighth century. The river was canalised in the 18th century, becoming part of the Grand Union Canal. Controlling the highway in this part of the East Midlands was of national importance. A castle was built at Mountsorrel in 1085, shortly after the Norman Conquest, to control the highway and possibly the river. During the Industrial Revolution, because of the poor state of the highway, canals were constructed throughout the British Isles, and the River Soar was opened in 1794 to convey goods to Leicester, while trade along the waterway on to the River Trent at Redhill had commenced in 1778. There were two main uses of the waterways: to convey coal for firing the steam pumps and engines, and to carry Mountsorrel granite for the construction of buildings. The granite was also used as crushed stone in the development of the highways. As the highways were improved, use of the canal system declined.

Today there is a resergence of canal use thanks to tourism and the use of canal boats as mobile homes. A 'slow' holiday, covering only a few miles per day, is a marvellous way to enjoy the very fine countryside of the East Midlands. A programme of expansion is currently taking place on the canals, with the construction of canal-side marinas.

A drawing of the locks on the Grand Union Canal near Barrow-upon-Soar, produced by Edward William Cooke in 1890.

Barrow-Upon-Soar

Industry Square and the war memorial in the 1920s at Barrow-upon-Soar.

On the roundabout with the road leading to Loughborough is a monument to a a plesiosaurus, one of the major finds uncovered in the local lime pit. It was a reptile that swam in the waters before the age of the dinosaurs. This photograph of the monument was taken in 2006. The preserved fossilised skeleton is on display at the New Walk Museum in Leicester.

Corbett's shop on the High Street in Barrow-upon-Soar in the early part of the 1920s. Tom Corbett was a local hairdresser.

Cotes Road in Barrow-upon-Soar in the 1930s.

The Boat House near the river bridge crossing the canalised River Soar in the 1920s.

A similar view taken a few years after the photograph printed above. Note the tea shop where canoes, boats and tents are for hire.

The river bridge crossing the Grand Union Canal, 2006.

A similar view of the river bridge taken in the 1930s.

The Riverside Inn, 14 Bridge Street, Barrow-upon-Soar, 2006. It was renamed the Boat House in 2009.

A fine drawing by William Edward Cooke of the bridge lock at Barrow-upon-Soar in 1880.

The Navigation Inn at Barrow-upon-Soar on Mill Lane, 2006. This inn was constructed to provide refreshment for the navvies that built the canal locks and bridges, and it continues to support the canal users. At the height of the boat trade in 1846 Thomas Oliver was the publican. Seventy years later, just after the end of World War One in 1918, Samuel Birch was the licensee.

A boat passing through the lock at 'Barrow Lock Bridge', number 29, in August 2006.

Soar Bridge Inn, 29 Bridge Street, Barrow-upon-Soar, 2006. It is situated very close to the bridge that gives it its name.

The Hammer & Pincers public house at Barrow-upon-Soar opened as a hostelry in 1753, and two cottages were incorporated into the main structure. The pub is situated on the junction of North Street and Church Lane. Between 1880 and 1916 it had four licensees: William King, Thomas Thorneycroft, Harry Lewis and Walter Smith.

'The Lock-up' at Barrow-upon-Soar, 2006. The building is octagonal with a pyramidal roof.

The Three Crowns public house, 6 Cotes Road, Barrow-upon-Soar, 2006. At the end of the 19th century it was run by two publicans, Thomas Briggs and William Brooks.

The sluice gates at Pilling's Lock near Barrow-upon-Soar control the River Soar and the depth of the navigation. This drawing was produced by William Edward Cooke in 1880.

Pilling's Lock, 2009. This modern marina has been excavated near the weir. A lock gate system has been connected to the Grand Union Canal.

The water mill at Barrow-upon-Soar from a drawing produced by William Edward Cooke in 1876. The mill was run by Henry Ward, who was also the licensee of the nearby Navigation Inn.

Barrow-upon-Soar water mill, c.1900. In the Domesday survey a water mill is indicated on this site. It had a long history of grinding corn, but in the early part of the 20th century it was grinding gypsum. Power was provided by two large waterwheels 15 and 20ft in diameter. The mill was demolished in 1938.

A photograph of the Mill House at Barrow-upon-Soar taken during the 1930s.

A photograph of Humphrey Perkins Grammar School, on Cotes Road, taken just before the commencement of World War One. Perkins founded a school here in 1717. Extensive alterations took place in the 1950s and were completed in 1955.

The Church of the Holy Trinity at Barrow-upon-Soar, in an engraving published by J.P. Malcolm in 1792.

A porringer given to the Church of the Holy Trinity in 1697 by Martha Utber, for use in the sacrament. A cover was added to this two-handled silver porringer in 1739.

The Church of the Holy Trinity at Barrow-upon-Soar, 2006.

An engraving published c.1800 of the Old Men's Hospital, founded by Humphrey Babington in 1686 and built in 1694.

The Old Men's Hospital opposite the Church of the Holy Trinity, 2009. The gateway to the building has Doric pilaster buttresses with a 'broken' pediment.

Within the forecourt is the entrance to the hospital, produced to a similar design to the main entrance.

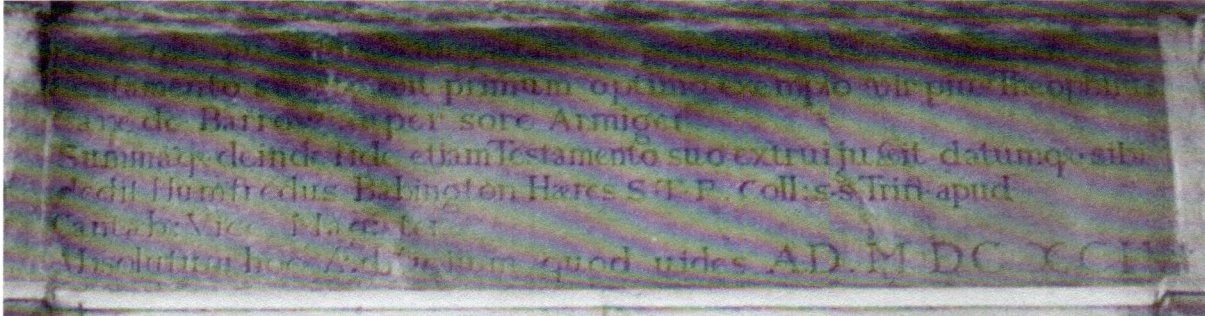

The inscription above the main entrance.

Quorn

The Village Hall at Quorn in 1904. The secretary was George White.

The bridge in the middle of Quorn in 1876. It crosses the loop of the River Soar that passes through the centre of the village. A wharf had been constructed leading from the Grand Union Canal. This drawing was produced by Edward William Cooke.

The Church of St Bartholomew, south-west view, from an engraving by J.P. Malcolm published in 1792. The building has a Perpendicular west tower.

A view of the Church of St Bartholomew taken in 2007. In the interior there are examples of Norman architecture. The most striking is the small Norman priest door.

The east view of the Church of St Bartholomew. In this church are numerous monuments to the Farnham family, who contributed much to the village. G.F. Farnham collated a fine collection of local history records in the early 20th century, and his manuscripts are held in the county record office at South Wigston.

Loughborough Road at Quorn in 1904.

The decorative iron bridge crossing the waterway leading to the wharf at Quorn, c.1910.

The decorative iron bridge at Quorn, 2009.

The coal wharf at Quorn in a drawing produced by William Edward Cooke in 1879.

The wharf at Quorn, off the Grand Union Canal, in 2009.

A farmyard off Wood Lane, Quorn. This drawing was published in 1880 as a lithograph, possibly drawn while the artist, William Edward Cooke, was living in the village in 1877.

Wood Lane, Quorn, c.1905.

The Manor House Hotel, Quorn, in 1922. Jasper A. Hartopp was the licensee.

The Manor House at Quorn, Woodhouse Road, 2007.

The Royal Oak Inn and the White Horse Hotel, c.1908. In front of the White Horse Hotel is parked a horse-drawn carrier cart offering goods for sale.

A photographic bird's-eye view of the various factories operating in Quorn just after World War One.

High Street, Quorn. In 1939 Richard Joyce was running the newsagent's shop at 25 High Street.

The White House public house at the junction of Station Road and Leicester Road in 2007. In 1904 the well-known licensee was William Farquhar Sheddon.

The Royal Oak at the junction of Meeting Street and High Street in 2007. In 1922 the Royal Oak was run by Ernest Winterton. Considerable alterations have been made to this building.

The Apple Tree public house is a 19th-century half-timbered building. In 1893 Thomas Chapman was the licensee.

The White Hart public house, 32 High Street, Quorn, 2007. James Ramsby was the licensee from the 1880s through to the 20th century. He was a local farmer and maltster, growing his own barley and brewing his own ale. Joseph Soar Storer was the owner in 1903, and by the outbreak of World War One Reuben Taylor was the licensee.

The Quorndon Fox, 46 High Street, Quorn, 2007. A splendid building recording the history of fox hunting in the East Midlands.

The Blacksmiths Arms public house, 29 Meeting Street, Quorn, 2007. In 1893 Henry Martin owned the building and possibly converted an adjacent cottage into the main building.

Quorn Hall and park, in an engraving published by William Walter in 1791. The hall was built in 1680 and became the home of Hugo Meynell in 1753. He died in 1808.

This postcard of Quorn Hall was posted from Quorn in 1911. The message is a note to a friend in Leicester. The sender, 'Emily', works at the hall and 'is very busy'. Two crosses indicate the servants' quarters where she sleeps.

Quorn Hall, c.1800, the home of Hugo Meynell. Meynell was considered to be a Derbyshire squire. Born on an estate at Bradley near Ashbourne in 1727, he inherited a considerable fortune. In his early 20s he decided that the development of the hunting of foxes was his life's ambition. He is known as the 'Father of Foxhunting' and bred what is considered the leading pack of hounds. The chasing of foxes through the rolling countryside of Nottinghamshire and Leicestershire was considered to be the height of fashion for the wealthy rich. It took the place of deer hunting after much of the local woodland had been cut for timber.

A photograph of Quorn Hall in 1940. It is now a hostel for Loughborough College. The hall was built in 1680 by Captain Henry Farnham.

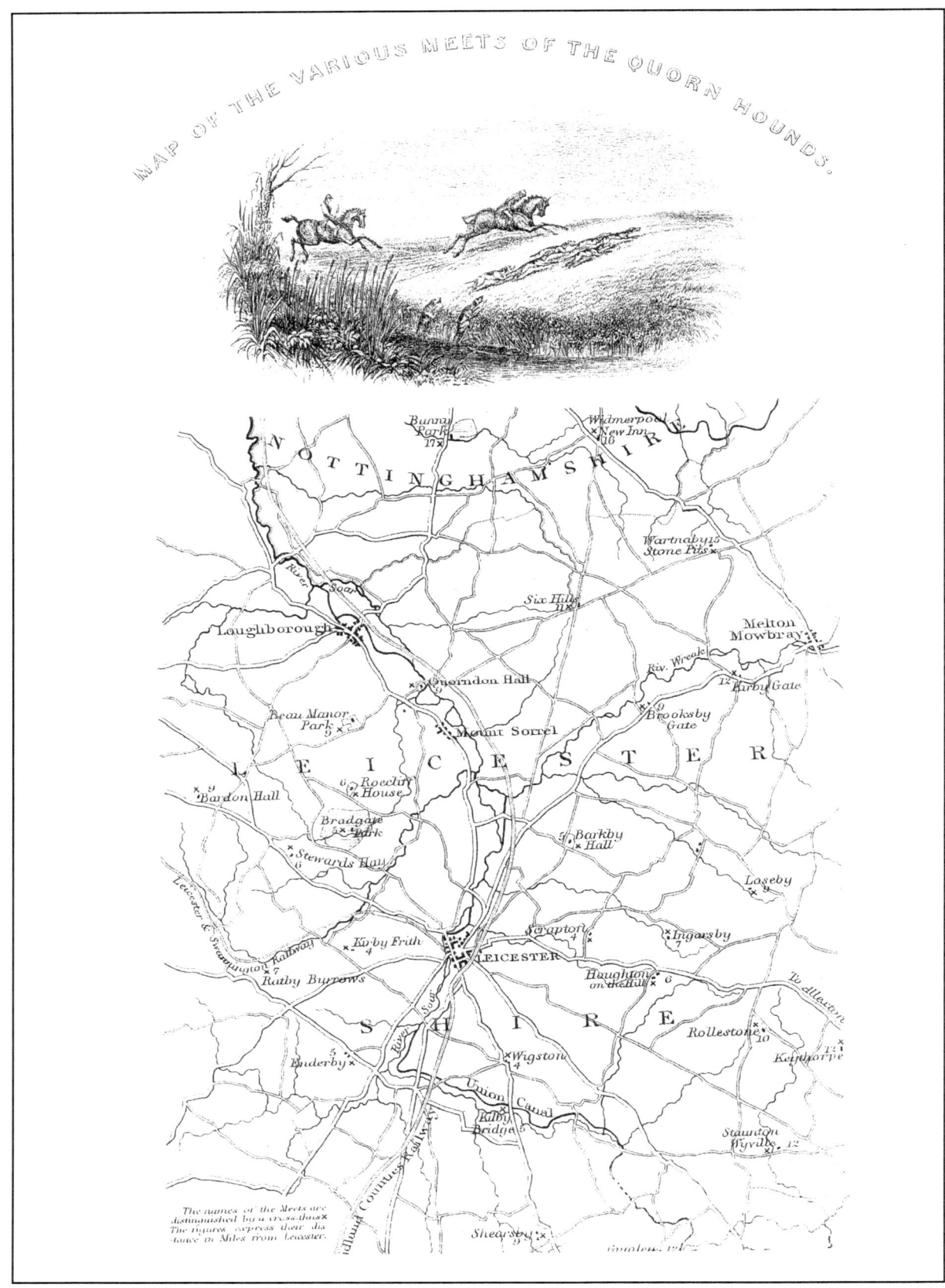

Published in 1847, this map shows the villages north of Leicester. Detailing the counties of Nottinghamshire and Leicestershire, it covers the area of countryside that was hunted by the Quorn Hounds. It was printed from an engraving by W. Hughes.

Quorn Hunt kennels, c.1900.

The entrance to the Quorn Hunt kennels, c.1905.

Mr Hugo Meynell (1753–1800), Master and founder of the Quorn Hunt, from a painting by Joshua Reynolds.

Tom Bishopp and Walter Keyte exercising the Quorn hounds, possibly in 1905.

A meeting of the Quorn Hunt at Quorn, c.1910. The Master of Foxhounds is Captain Frank Forester.

The Quorn Hunt kennels at Quorn in 1878 in a drawing by William Edward Cooke. There is a possibility that this is Tom Firr, the famous huntsman, feeding his favourite foxhound.

A photograph taken at the Quorn Hunt kennels, c.1900. This may be Tom Bishopp feeding his favourite foxhound.

WILLIAM MARSHALL, EARL OF PEMBROKE, WHO LED THE UNSUCCESSFUL BESIEGING FORCE ON MOUNTSORREL CASTLE, 1217, ON BEHALF OF THE KING. THE SIEGE WAS LIFTED WHEN THE KING'S MEN WERE THREATENED BY THE COMBINED FRENCH AND BARONIAL ARMY.

The monument and commemorative plaque to William Marshall, Earl of Pembroke, guardian to Henry III, who succeeded to the throne at the age of nine. This powerful earl ran the country on his behalf from 1216 to 1219.

Richard I (1189–99). The son of Henry II, he led the Third Crusade to Jerusalem. He seldom visited England but on one occasion he lived for a time at Mountsorrel Castle and made considerable improvements to its defences.

Henry III (1216–72) succeeded his father at the age of nine and was influenced by William Marshall as his guardian. He was a weak king and the barons rebelled against him. Simon de Montfort defeated him in battle and then ruled the country until his son, Edward I, killed de Montfort.

Castle Hill, Mountsorrel, from an engraving published in 1757 by J. Royce. A castle was built on this hill by Hugh Lupus, Earl of Chester, in about 1085 to control the river valley north of Leicester. It was in the possession of the Earls of Leicester from about 1140. During the reign of Stephen it withstood numerous attacks during the baronial wars. In the period 1173–74 it was held by Prince Henry, who was in revolt against his father Henry II, who took the castle after a lengthy siege. Richard I fortified the building and built an extensive tower and hall from local stone. The castle came under the control of Saer de Quincy against King John during the barons' war of 1215, and in 1217 William Marshall, Earl of Pembroke, besieged the castle on behalf of Henry III. The castle at that time was held by a group of baronial mercenaries under the leadership of Ranulf, Earl of Chester. After the Battle of Lincoln in 1217, the king ordered this castle to be destroyed, describing it as 'a nest of the Devil and a Den of Thieves'.

A drawing of the Market Cross at Mountsorrel produced by William Edward Cooke in 1880.

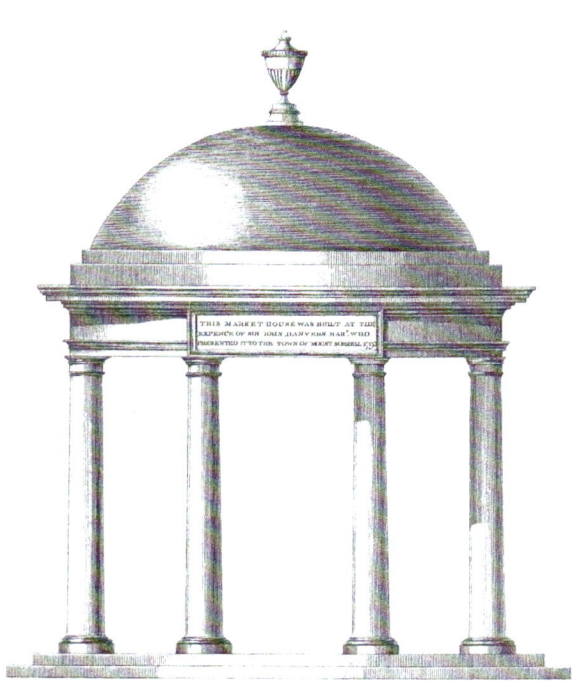

An engraving published in 1800, showing an engraved plaque positioned on the cupola. 'This market house was built at the expense of Sir John Danvers Bart, who presented it to the town of Mount Sorrell, 1793'.

A photograph of the cupola taken just after World War One.

The Old Butter Market at Mountsorrel, c.1900. This was the Market Cross where goods were marketed, with particular emphasis on butter and cheese made locally by the farmers' wives.

Visitors at the Market Cross, August 2003.

A photograph of the Market Cross at Mountsorrel, with a group of children outside the Co-operative Society shop, c.1910.

The castle hill at Mountsorrel, c.1910.

The south-east view of Castle Hill, Mountsorrel, c.1800.

The remains of Mountsorrel Castle, viewed from the village in the 1790s. In March 1643 Royalists used this as a defensive position during a skirmish in the Civil War. Hastings's troops from Ashby de la Zouch fought through the village with a Roundhead force from Leicester and retreated to the ruined castle.

The World War One memorial, designed by Shirley Harrison, was erected on the site of Mountsorrel Castle in 1926. This Leicestershire battle site is well worth visiting on a sunny summer day, to enjoy the views and attempt to understand the importance of this site in the baronial wars of the 12th and 13th century, and the 17th-century Civil War.

Children sitting on the edge of the escarpment overlooking the Soar Valley across Mountsorrel, summer 2003.

The site of Mountsorrel Castle, 2001. Exposed Mountsorrel granite was extensively mined in the area, and natural stone was used in the construction of the original castle. Stonemasons employed by Richard I reinforced the existing castle. Carefully laid granite floors can still be found in the grassed areas of the ruined castle.

Visitors sitting on the exposed granite remains on the summit of Mountsorrel Castle, summer 2003.

A view of Castle Hill at Mountsorrel from the River Soar c.1910.

The Soar Valley from Castle Hill, Mountsorrel, summer 2003.

The River Soar viewed from Castle Hill with the village of Mountsorrel in the foreground, c.1920.

*Shirley Harrison's splendid war
memorial on Castle Hill at
Mountsorrel, summer 2003.*

*The beacon, Mountsorrel Castle,
2003. After the young King Henry
III gave instructions in 1217 to the
Earl of Pembroke, his guardian, to
demolish this castle, the stone was
plundered and mining took place
in and near the bailey.*

The water mill at Mountsorrel in 1912, the year it ceased operating. Flour was ground by power generated from two wheels, 12.5ft in diameter. In the mill there were four pairs of French stones and two pairs of Peak stones.

Mountsorrel water mill, 1912. The mill fell into disrepair in 1940, when the top of the mill was removed. In 1960, the whole mill was demolished.

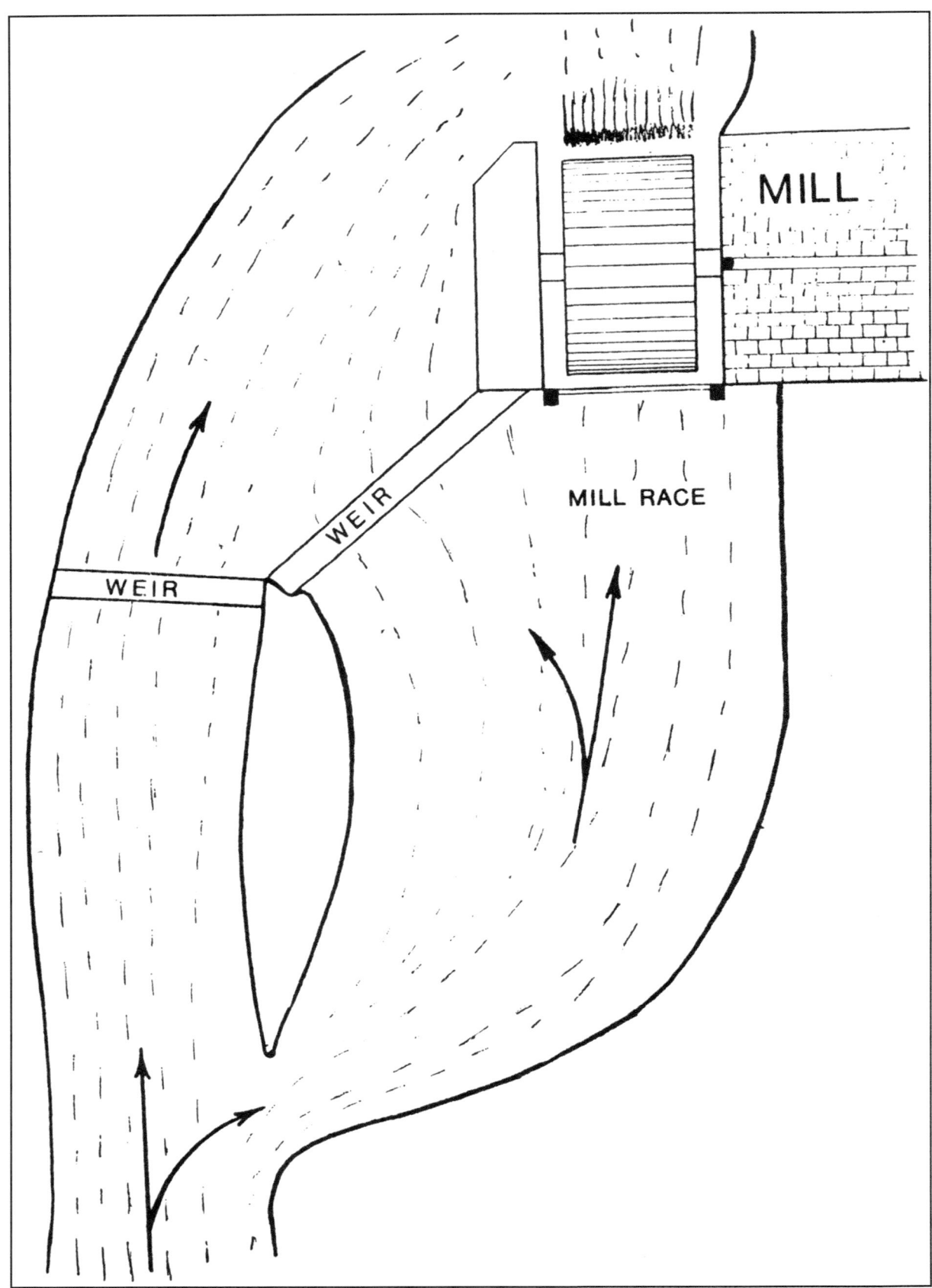

In this drawing the flow of water along the River Soar is indicated. The height of the mill pond/race is controlled by a weir. The flow of water turns the wheel.

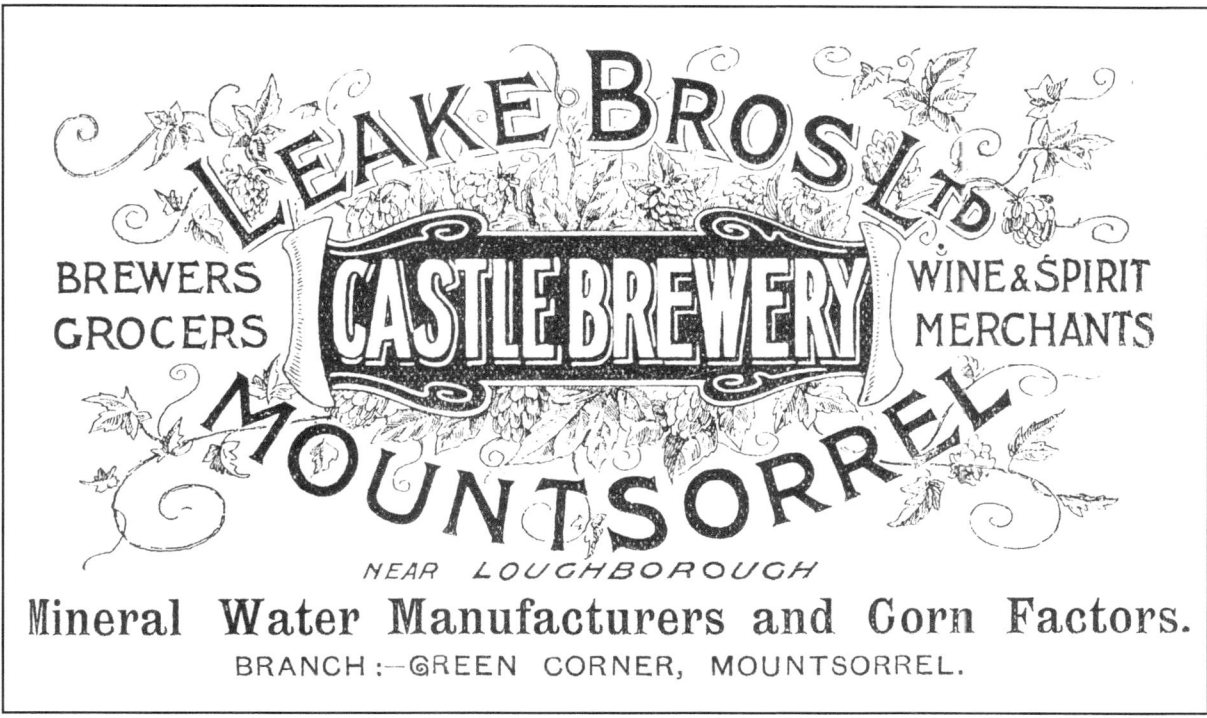

An advertisement for a brewery operating near the village green in the centre of Mountsorrel in 1904.

This photograph of the village green at Mountsorrel was published in about 1905.

Thatched cottages on the village green, c.1910, with Christ Church in the background.

A general store run by Charles William Rudkin in 1916, leading to The Green.

The Church of St Peter, Mountsorrel. This is the north-east view, showing the mediaeval tower, in an engraving by J.P. Malcolm.

A silver cup and silver cover paten given to the mediaeval Church of St Peter, Mountsorrel, in 1574.

Mountsorrel Granite Company excavating stone in 1905. It was used as crushed stone for tarmacadam and in the manufacture of kerb and paving stones.

The weir at the Grand Union Canal in Mountsorrel, 2009.

The Echo Bridge crossing the Grand Union Canal at Mountsorrel in 1910. The opening of this canal in about 1812 promoted the growth of the granite mining industry. In 1860 this fine bridge was built to carry crushed granite to the Midland Railway at Barrow-upon-Soar.

Echo Bridge in the spring of 2009.

The King William IV public house, situated on the main highway through the village in 2009. In 1846 John Brown was the licensee. This building was also registered as a post office.

The historic entrance to the yard at the rear of the King William IV public house. To carry the post during the stagecoach years the licensee held a 'Royal Licence'. The coach would change horses, collect and deliver the mail and take on passengers.

The Stag and Pheasant public house at Mountsorrel, 2009. Three notable licensees held the licence: John Hewett in 1877, Thomas Green in 1916 and John Hickling in 1922.

The Swan Inn public house on the main road through the village, 2009.

The wharf at Mountsorrel with the Church of St Peter in the background. This drawing was produced by William Edward Cooke in 1880.

Another drawing of the wharf at Mountsorrel, with the Church of St Peter in the background, drawn by William Edward Cooke and published in 1880. William Cad's barge dealing off the wharf stands in the basin.

A barge entering the locks at Mountsorrel, summer 2003.

Opening the lock gates on the Grand Union Canal at Mountsorrel, summer 2007.

The lock gates are open, 2003.

The locks on the Grand Union Canal at Mountsorrel in 1880, in a drawing by William Edward Cooke. Stables are situated on the right, while the lock keeper's cottage is on the left. Thomas Carr was the lock keeper.

A barge entering the locks at Mountsorrel in 2003. The stables on the right have been converted into the Waterside Inn.

Villages to the West
Garendon Park

To the west of Loughborough is Garendon Park, the site of a Cistercian abbey from 1134. Henry VIII dissolved the abbey in 1536 and the estate and buildings were granted to the Duke of Rutland, but the family sold the estate and holdings to Sir Ambrose Phillipps in 1684. He had interests in Shepshed, Dishley and Hathern, and if you visit these villages evidence of his ownership is very clear in the churches and in the names of the village streets. Before the abbey was erected there is evidence that a village existed in the Garendon Park area, and in the future a new village will be built on the site. Hopefully this will incorporate the monument erected by one of the Phillipps family. A former mansion owned by the estate was demolished in 1964.

The Cistercian monks would have run a farming estate, and the present family manage an area of extensive farmland throughout the north-west of Loughborough. A Dishley farm was connected with Garendon Abbey in the 12th century and the association continued when it was owned by the Phillipps family. They also owned and ran Dishley Grange, the home of the famous farmer Robert Bakewell (1725–95).

Garendon Abbey. An engraving by William Walker, published in 1791 before extensive alterations had taken place.

Garendon Abbey/Hall in an engraving from a drawing made in 1795 by Longmate.

Garendon Hall viewed from across the lake in the 1920s.

Garendon Hall in an engraving produced by James Basire in 1801. This was the home of Thomas March Phillipps.

Garendon Hall in all its glory. This photograph was taken at the end of the 1920s. In 1841 A.W.N. Pugin proposed changes to the original hall. From 1864–66 E.W. Pugin gave instructions for many alterations to the original plans held by the then owner, Ambrose Lisle March Phillipps de Lisle.

A 15th-century Cistercian Monk of Garendon Abbey with his cowl, from an engraving published in 1800.

A 15th-century Cistercian Monk of Garendon Abbey without his cowl.

The 'Blackbrook' in Garendon Park, in a drawing produced by William Edward Cooke in 1883.

The Triumphal Arch in Garendon Park, c.1930. This magnificent arch was erected near the entrance to the park on the Ashby Road on the instructions of Ambrose Phillipps, who was influenced by the magnificent Roman remains he encountered on his grand tour in the 1730s.

The Arch of Trajan at Acona, Italy c.1930. Ambrose Phillipps toured Italy in the 1730s. Obviously a very wealthy individual, on his return he commenced erecting 'follies' throughout his park. His famous arch was erected over the remains of a mediaeval building, possibly the site of an early manor house, part of the deserted mediaeval village site.

An engraving detailing the carvings incorporated in the Triumphal Arch in Garendon Park, 1801.

An engraving of the Temple of Venus in Garendon Park, 1801.

The Temple of Venus, Garendon Park, 1904. This Grade II listed building has been considerably damaged by thieves removing the lead roof. In 2009 the trustees were in the process of covering the domed roof in stainless steel.

In Garendon Park stands an obelisk constructed from rendered brick, photographed here c.1920. One of Ambrose Phillipps's constructions, it was influenced by Cleopatra's Needle, erected on the Thames Embankment in London.

The packhorse bridge that crosses the Blackbrook, 1905. It stands on the route from Dishley Grange to Garendon Abbey, and it was possibly erected in around 1135, at the time the Cistercian Abbey was built.

The packhorse bridge in Garendon Park, 1993.

A squadron of the Leicester Imperial Yeomanry on parade in Garendon Park, 1904.

The Lincolnshire Regiment at camp in Garendon Park, 1909.

Shepshed is a very large village that perhaps should be classed as a small town. It was the site of a mediaeval village market, and in this 2002 photograph the farmers' market is in full swing. The name of this village in the 1840s was Sheepshead, by 1860 it was Sheepshed and in 1900 the 'e' was dropped and it became Shepshed. The lord of the manor in the 1840s was Charles March Phillipps of Garendon Park.

Stalls in the farmers' market at Shepshed in 2002.

Charnwood Road in Shepshed in the 1930s.

Sullington Road in Shepshed in the 1930s.

Forest Street in Shepshed in the 1930s.

The Market Place, Shepshed, 2002.

The Market Place, Shepshed, in 1911 with the Church of St Botolph high in the background.

The Red Lion, 2009. In 1840 William Bennett was the landlord, and in the 1860s Thomas Clarke was the licensee. He ran the pub for over 20 years, also raising cattle on rented farmland to be marketed from his butchers shop.

The Crown, 2009. From the 1840s until the 1870s Thomas Poyner ran this public house. In about 1880 Robert Cotton, a farmer, took over the inn for the rest of the century.

The Crown in 2009.

The Blue Ball, 2009. From the middle of the 19th century until the early 20th century this public house was run by Swift Gadd, Thomas Keightley, Thomas Staton and James Powdrill.

The Britannia Inn, 2009. William Blake was licensee in 1840, followed by Robert Burdett Colton in the 1850s, who ran the hostelry for over 10 years. Thomas Webster then ran the pub until the 1890s when Henry Hoyes took over.

The Old Crown Restaurant, 2002. As a public house it was run by Stanfield Dalby in 1840, Edward Thomas Hutchinson in 1872 and Miss Clara Bonser in 1899.

The Church of St Botolph in an engraving published c.1790. The church has a 13th-century tower.

A cup given to Sheepshead Church in 1687 by Lady Phillipps of Garendon Park.

A two-handled silver cup with cover presented to Sheepshead Church in 1749 by Revd Thomas Heath MA.

The Church of St Botolph, Shepshed, c.1920.

The Church of St Botolph, Shepshed, 2009.

St Winefride's Catholic Church, Garendon Road, Shepshed, March 2009.

The main entrance to St Winefride's Church. This church was built during the years 1927–28 to a design by Alan D. Reid. In the church is a high altar designed in 1842 by Pugin.

Shepshed Windmill, which was converted into a private house in 1958–59.

Shepshed Windmill, c.1934. This windmill was built by J. Bramley in 1841–45. In 1889 the mill was owned and run by Henry Draper, who continued to grind corn in the mill until 1935. It ceased operating and gradually fell into disrepair. By 1950 it had lost its cap. In 1958 the cap and sails were replaced. It is now a private house.

Shepshed Windmill in 1978.

The dam at Black Brook Reservoir, near the windmill south-west of Shepshed, 1910.

Dishley

The church at Dishley (north-east view). Drawn by Schnebbelie, it was engraved by Liparoti and published in 1790. This was the mediaeval Saxon church, which was constructed to support what is now the deserted village of Dishley. The small village was purchased by Garendon Abbey in the 14th century. The Cistercians evicted the peasants and laid out the area to form a large grange to raise cattle, sheep and grow corn.

The church at Dishley (south-west view), in an engraving published in 1796.

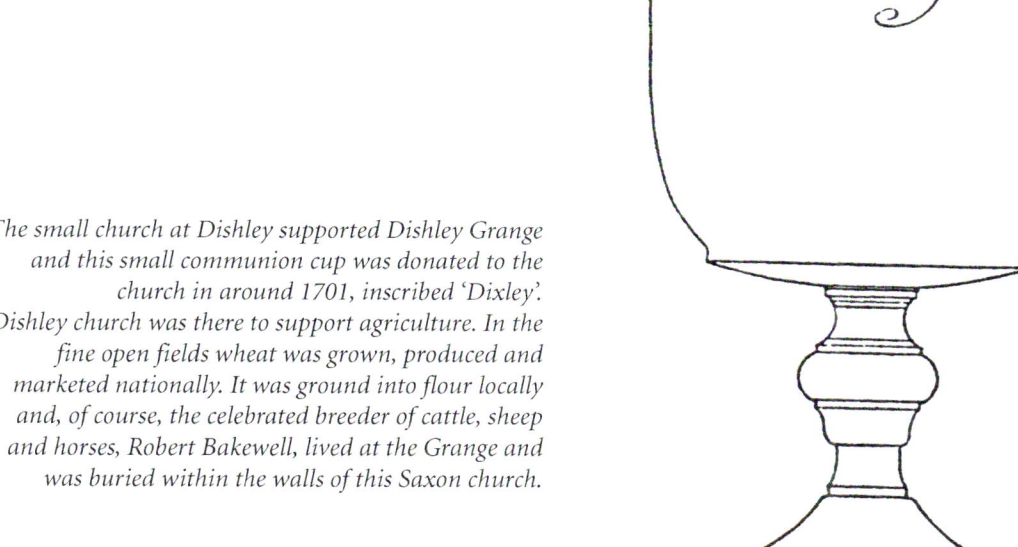

The ruins of Dishley Church. William Edward Cooke visited the ruined building in 1880 and produced this drawing of the deconsecrated church.

The small church at Dishley supported Dishley Grange and this small communion cup was donated to the church in around 1701, inscribed 'Dixley'. Dishley church was there to support agriculture. In the fine open fields wheat was grown, produced and marketed nationally. It was ground into flour locally and, of course, the celebrated breeder of cattle, sheep and horses, Robert Bakewell, lived at the Grange and was buried within the walls of this Saxon church.

Dishley water mill in 1880, drawn by William Edward Cooke.

Dishley water mill in 1904.

Dishley water mill, c.1890. This water mill was constructed in the extensive farm land to the north of Loughborough. There are two water mills listed in the Domesday Book, one of which may have been on the site of the mill at Dishley. This mill was important for supplying flour to the Cistercian Abbey at Garendon, and the estate became part of the farming empire controlled by the Cistercians in the 12th century.

The wheel and wheelhouse, c.1890. According to published records it would seem this water mill ceased grinding corn in 1904.

The Dishley water mill converted into two cottages, 1975.

Robert Bakewell (1725–95) was considered to be the leading breeder of livestock in the 18th century. He bred and improved the Leicester ram and the Midland Longhorn; made improvements in the growing and storing of arable crops; and improved the carthorse, cross-breeding it with West Friesland mares.

A Midland Longhorn, a breed originally established by Robert Bakewell.

A Bakewell Ewe, developed at Dishley, in an engraving published in 1790.

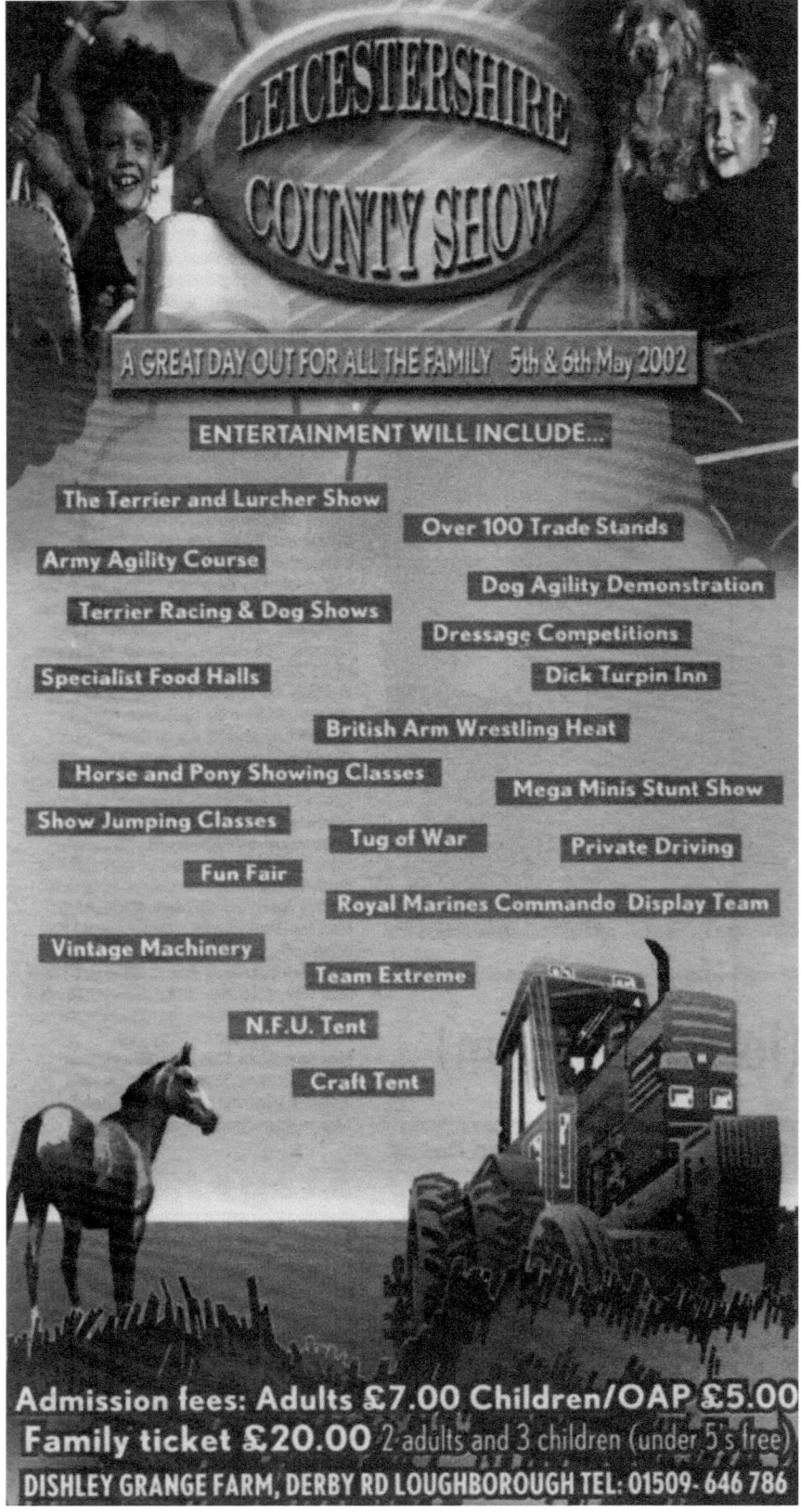

The poster for the 161st County Show of the Leicestershire Agricultural Society, 2002. Many venues have been chosen over the past 150 years. For 11 years the show was held, appropriately, at Dishley Grange. It is now held on a deserted airfield south of Melton Mowbray.

It is interesting to see horses being ridden in the ring. Robert Bakewell was interested in breeding speciality horses in the 18th century.

The show celebrates agriculture, farm stock and horses.

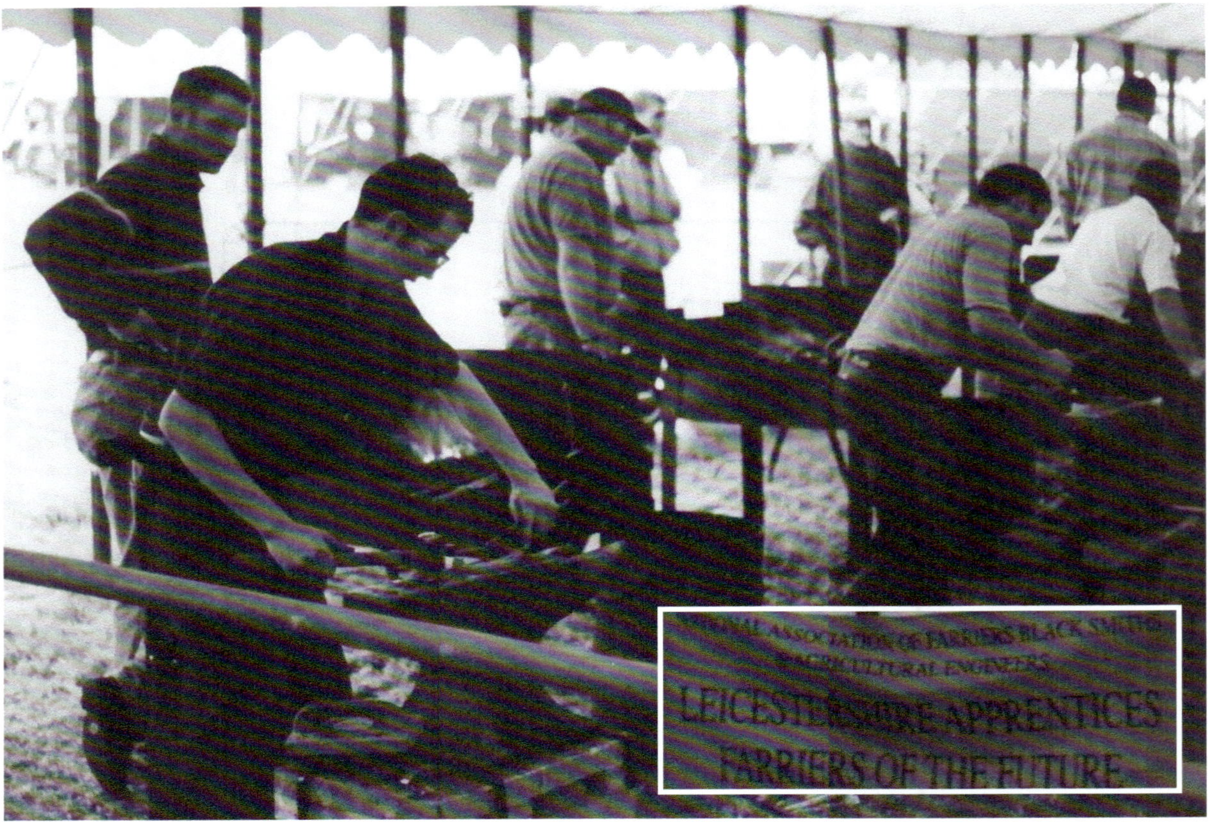

LEICESTERSHIRE APPRENTICES
FARRIERS OF THE FUTURE

Three photographs showing a competition organised by the National Association of Farriers. A group of local apprentices are competing to produce the finest horseshoe from a piece of base metal.

The Westerby Bassett Hounds with Master of Hounds Mrs A.E. Burton, 2002.

Steve Barrow, whipper-in for the Atherstone Hunt, leading the pack of hounds across the main ring.

The 1st Regiment of Royal Horse Artillery on display, 2002. This is an L118-/05 MM Light Gun of British design, first used in the 1970s, particularly during the Falklands War.

The 9th/12th Royal Lancers, 2002. This is a light tank used by this regiment as a recce vehicle. Called the 'Sabre', it is armed with a 30mm Rardon cannon.

A Massey Ferguson leading the parade of vintage tractors, 2002.

Terrier racing in the main ring, 2002.

The Market Cross at Hathern, August 2006. This is a very well preserved market cross. On such central sites the people living in and around the village would hold their weekly market.

The Anchor Inn, Loughborough Road, Hathern, 2006. This public house was in the ownership of John Cooper from 1860 until the 1890s. In 1899 Albert Cooper was the licensee.

The Dew Drop. In 1880 Frederick Price was the licensee. The pub was given this name because a local retired farm worker visited the inn every day, sitting near the fire and, as a joke, the pub was named after this local character who had a permanent cold. Today a modern sign hangs on the edge of the highway. In the 1940s Mrs Clifton ran the public house, and the name of the pub was greeted with much amusement by visiting American soldiers.

The Hathern Market Cross, 1886, drawn by William Edward Cooke. The 13th-century Church of St Peter stands in the background, and behind the cross is a dilapidated thatched cottage.

Hathern Market Cross in 1905. The roof of the thatched cottage had been repaired. The manor of Hathern was purchased by Ambrose Phillipps in 1683. Phillipps would have obtained income in a form of taxation on goods sold at this market.

Hathern Parish School, opened 11 February 1850. John Baracle was schoolmaster. This lithograph was produced by the printer to Queen Victoria, Day & Son of London.

Hathern Market Cross in an engraving published in 1790. Village markets such as the one at Hathern continued well into the 19th century, controlled by the elected village constable or by the Church. In 1894 parish councils were created and most village markets ceased to exist after this date.

Mediaeval markets were held on agreed days or on high days and holidays. Items for trade and produce for sale were stacked on or around the steps constructed around the base of the religious cross. Haggling would proceed, prices would be challenged and bartering would take place. A few villages still retain the legal right to hold markets, which would have been granted by the monarch.

South-east view of the Church of St Peter in an engraving by J.P. Malcolm published in 1792.

The Church of St Peter, Hathern, 1914.

Cross Street, Hathern, c.1920.

The Three Crowns public house on Wide Lane, 2006. The licensees were: 1846 John Robinsor, 1862 William Cox, 1885 Edwin Caldwell and 1889 George Wells. During World War One Henry Randon was the publican.

'Eaves' and the Woods

Make a journey south-east off the road at Quorn and you enter a most picturesque part of the East Midlands. Woodhouse is a delightful village with a collection of beautiful houses. To the north-east of the village is Beaumanor Hall, an incredible building constructed in 1845–47 by Robert Herrick, to a Jacobean design by William Railton. Purchased by Leicestershire County Council in the 1960s, today it serves many purposes, hosting educational conferences, weddings and other events. To the east of the village is some fine rolling countryside and farmland, with exposed granite features dotting the landscape. Woodhouse Eaves is an interesting village, and you can drive around the lanes and enjoy nearby Beacon Hill Country Park, an Iron Age encampment. The Church of St Paul is also worth visiting, standing on 'the rocks' with a cave underneath it. It is a Victorian building, also built to a design by William Railton in 1837.

An engraving published in 1791 from a drawing produced near Woodhouse with Woodhouse Eaves in the distance and the windmill on the hill.

Woodhouse

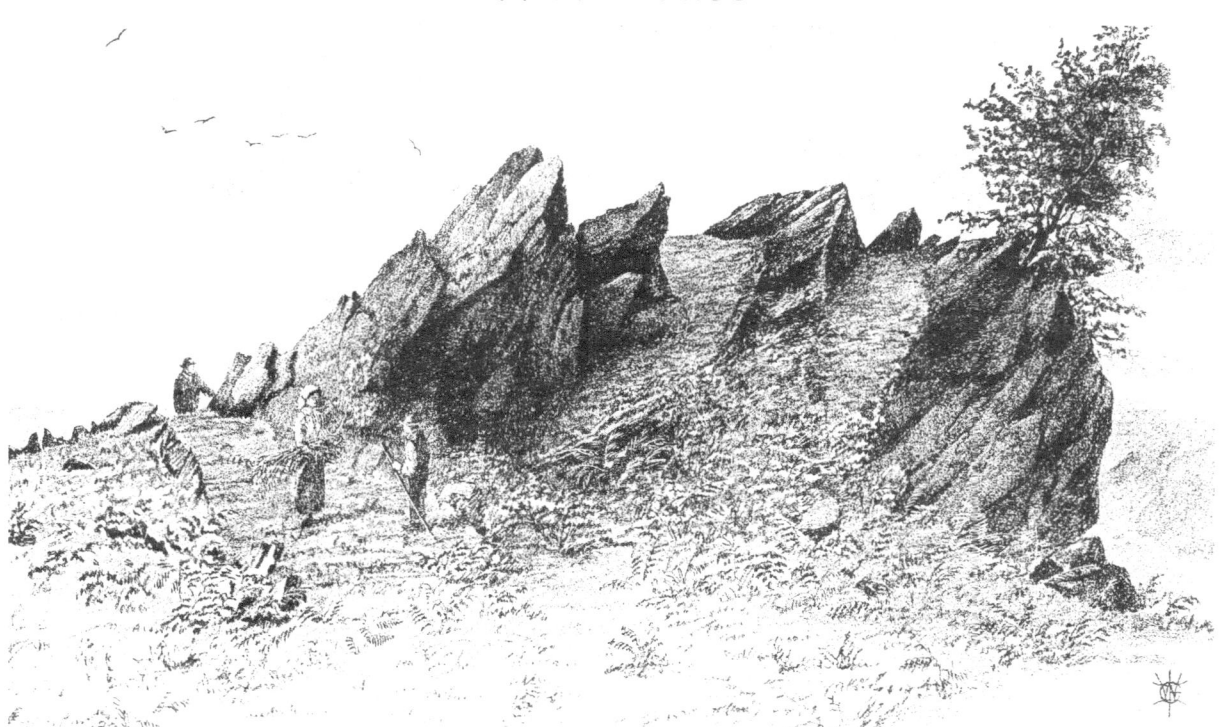

A drawing of rocks in Pocketgate, Hangingstone Hills, in 1887. William Edward Cooke must have loved walking in this area when he lived at Loughborough.

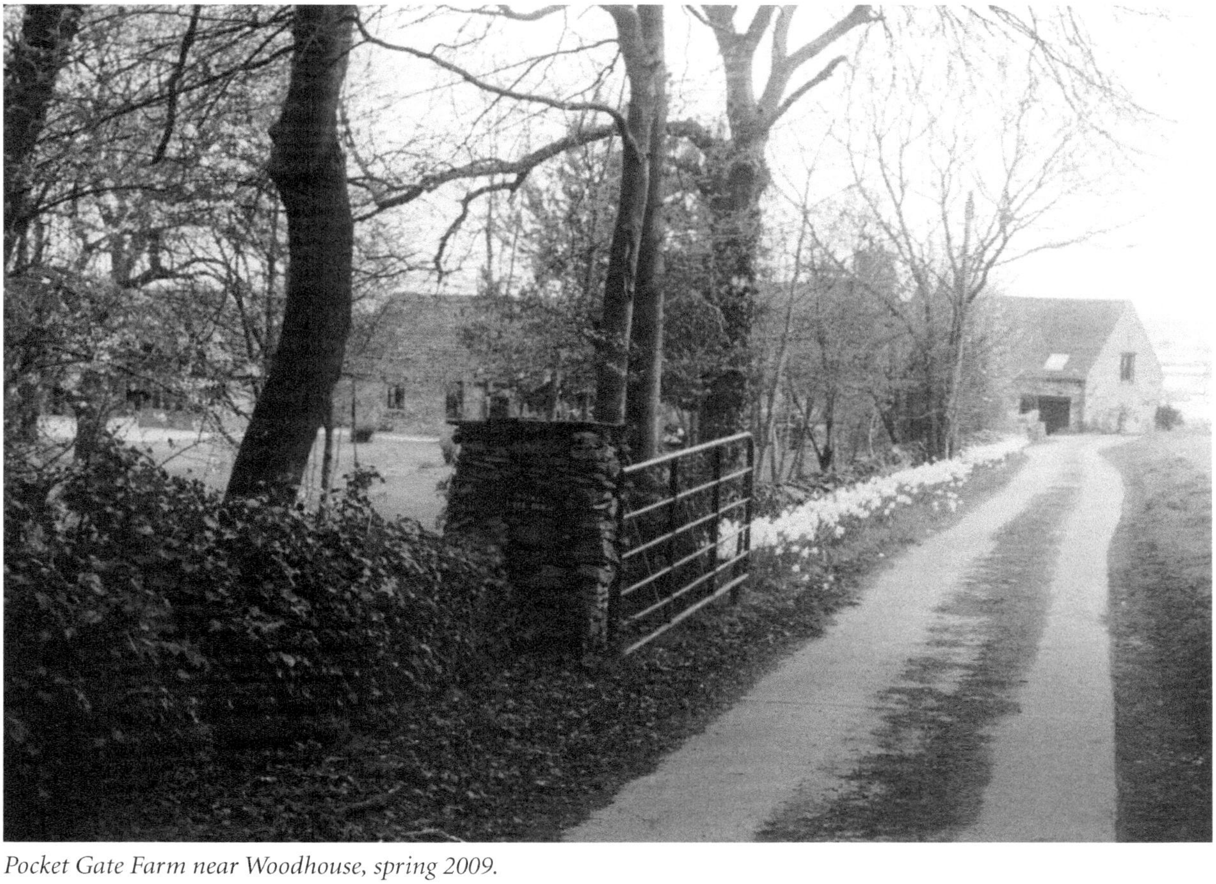

Pocket Gate Farm near Woodhouse, spring 2009.

The fountain at Woodhouse, 1903.

The Woodhouse Fountain in 2009. A public drinking fountain financed and constructed on the instructions of William Perry Herrick in 1858, the iron 'Bull's Head' that delivers the flowing water was cast in John William Taylor's Loughborough bell foundry. The fountain was refurbished in 2000 in celebration of the Millennium.

'Old Woodhouse' on the road leading to the Brand and Swithland, 1908.

'Old Woodhouse', spring 2009.

Beaumanor Hall in an engraving by William Walker, September 1791. The home of William Herrick, it was a classical mansion built by John Westley in 1725–27.

Beaumanor Hall in a drawing engraved by T. Prattent in 1798. This magnificent building was demolished in 1841.

Beaumanor Hall at Woodhouse drawn by William Edward Cooke in 1890, 43 years after it was rebuilt.

Beaumanor Hall viewed from the park, 1988.

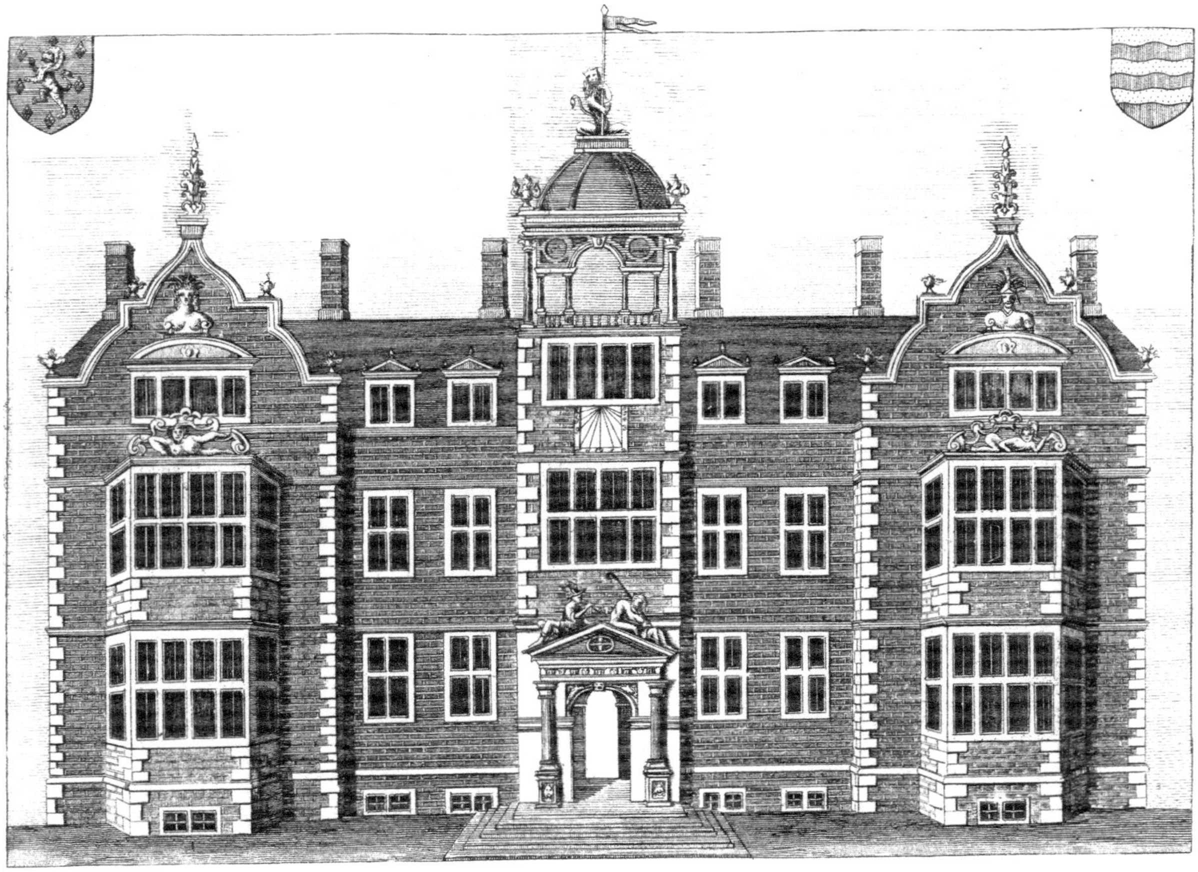

Beaumanor Hall, the home of the Herrick family after 1845.

Beaumanor Hall in the spring of 2009. It is now owned by Leicestershire County Council, who purchased it from the War Office, who had purchased it from the Herricks in 1947.

The Church of St Mary-in-the-Elms at Woodhouse. The name of the village means 'houses in the woods'. A church stood on this site in the 14th century. The Victorians completely demolished and rebuilt this building in 1878.

A charming drawing of the Church of St Mary at Woodhouse
published by William Edward Cooke in 1880.

This is an interesting silver cup donated to St Mary's Church in
1610, with an engraved coat of arms: fess vairé or and gules,
crest a head argent, attired sable, gorged with a wreath. They
are the arms of Sir William Herrick of Beaumanor Park. An
inscription reads: Virtus nobilititat Gulielmus Hericke Miles
Amoris ergo dedit 1610.

The south-east view of the Church of St Mary at Woodhouse in an engraving by Schnebbelie from a drawing by W. Cook published in May 1791.

North-east view of the Church of St Mary at Woodhouse, in an engraving published by T. Prattent in 1792.

Woodhouse Eaves

The Church of St Paul at Woodhouse Eaves in 2007. Built in local stone and slate by William Railton in 1837, the church stands high above an old slate quarry.

An 1880 drawing by William Edward Cooke. The remains of buildings used in the mining of slate are visible to the right and left of the drawing.

The Church of St Paul at Woodhouse Eaves in 1914. The cave under the church was formed by mining for slate.

The cave and church at Woodhouse Eaves just before World War Two.

The cave at Woodhouse Eaves, 2007.

The Wheatsheaf public house, 90 Brand Hill, Woodhouse Eaves, 2007. In 1880, the landlady was Mrs Mary Dable. From 1900 to 1916 it was run by William Clarke and in 1940 Richard Hipwell was landlord.

The Wheatsheaf, 2007. Obviously a coaching inn, the entrance to the yard still exists. The building is constructed from local stone and slate.

The Main Street, Woodhouse Eaves, 1907, with the Church of St Peter high in the background. The vicar was Revd Arnold James Watkinson Hiley MA, of Exeter College, Oxford.

A general view of Woodhouse Eaves, with the windmill high in the background, c.1910.

The Curzon Arms, 44 Maplewell Road, 2007. Samuel Isaac Preston was the licensee from World War One until World War Two.

The Pear Tree public house situated on Church Hill, Woodhouse Eaves, 2007. John Mayes was landlord in 1916 and Leslie Walker was the landlord in 1940.

Woodhouse Eaves Windmill, which was owned by the Beaumanor Estate. This post mill was built in Derbyshire and erected on the hill near the village. John Hives was running the mill in 1863, but in 1895 the mill was badly damaged. It was never repaired for the use of grinding corn.

Woodhouse Eaves Windmill, c.1920. It was made safe by 1900 and became a feature on many postcards.

The picturesque windmill at Woodhouse Eaves was destroyed by fire in 1945.

The stone base of the mill at Woodhouse Eaves in 1978.

A drawing of rocks at Pocketgate near Woodhouse 1890. A fine illustration by Edward Cooke.

Conclusion

I have compiled this collection of images of the town of Loughborough and the surrounding villages as a personal journey. I have always been interested in how weekly markets must have influenced the local populace. Markets would have been very important to the well-being of the local inhabitants. The site where markets were held is still well recorded. During the mediaeval period, without them village life would have been very difficult. Goods were displayed around 'the cross' and sold and bartered. This is an engraving of a 17th-century lady on the way to market. Possibly the wife of the local squire or local merchant, she would have paid for her goods with cash. Money was always in short supply to the working class during the mediaeval and Tudor periods. Today Loughborough market still flourishes, although, in the 21st century, supermarkets have taken the place of the mediaeval weekly market. I hope you have enjoyed this selection of drawings, engravings, photographs and text about Loughborough and the surrounding area.

Trevor Hickman

BV - #0127 - 280426 - C0 - 276/195/12 - PB - 9781780914060 - Gloss Lamination